Stalking

Focus on Contemporary Issues (FOCI) addresses the pressing problems, ideas and debates of the new millennium. Subjects are drawn from the arts, sciences and humanities, and are linked by the impact they have had or are having on contemporary culture. FOCI books are intended for an intelligent, alert audience with a general understanding of, and curiosity about, the intellectual debates shaping culture today. Instead of easing readers into a comfortable awareness of particular fields, these books are combative. They offer points of view, take sides and are written with passion.

SERIES EDITORS
Barrie Bullen and Peter Hamilton

In the same series

Cool Rules
Dick Pountain and David Robins

Chromophobia
David Batchelor

Global Dimensions
John Rennie Short

Celebrity
Chris Rojek

Activism!
Tim Jordan

Animal
Erica Fudge

Dreamtelling
Pierre Sorlin

Anarchism
Seán M. Sheehan

The Happiness Paradox
Ziyad Marar

First Peoples
Jeffrey Sissons

Contemporary Gothic
Catherine Spooner

Retro
Elizabeth E. Guffey

Stalking

BRAN NICOL

REAKTION BOOKS

To Karen, Joe and Jamie, with love

Published by Reaktion Books Ltd
33 Great Sutton Street
London EC1V 0DX, UK

www.reaktionbooks.co.uk

First published 2006

Printed and bound in Great Britain
by Cromwell Press, Trowbridge, Wiltshire

British Library Cataloguing in Publishing Data
Nicol, Bran, 1969–
    Stalking. - (Focus on contemporary issues)
    1.Stalking
    I.Title
    158.2

    ISBN-13: 978 1 86189 289 8
    ISBN-10: 1 86189 289 6

Contents

Introduction

Stalking is, paradoxically, both a new and an old phenomenon. Scarcely a week goes by without a lurid tale of stalking appearing in at least one of the tabloids. Numerous cases of stalking are considered by the courts every year. Celebrities have come to recognize that the price of fame is often to find oneself stalked. Yet the fact is that people have always threatened, persecuted, attacked, desired and become infatuated with each other. This, lamentably, is part of being human. One of the tasks of this book is to show that 'stalking' has been part of the cultural consciousness – and unconscious – for almost two hundred years, as demonstrated by its depiction in literary texts, films, artworks, news reports, television programmes, comic strips, pop songs, etc. But something *has* changed over the last couple of decades. Either we are more obsessive and hostile towards each other now, or maybe just more *anxious* about certain kinds of intimate relationships. Whichever, the outcome is that a new label has emerged to designate these troubling forms of human interaction. It is only in the last five years or so that 'stalking' or 'stalker' have become everyday terms. Before the early 1990s we wouldn't have been using them at all.

This book will try to explain why stalking has become so prominent over the past few decades. It will claim that although stalking is indisputably an old form of behaviour it is no accident that it was only in the 1990s that it became defined, pathologized and criminalized. Stalking is symptomatic of currents that characterize late twentieth and early twenty-first-century culture. Perhaps there is even something about our society that *produces* stalking. Crucial here is the distinctive double-helix that makes our culture what it is: the power of the mass media to shape our experience of reality, and our fascination with celebrity and the way it massages our yearning for intimacy. Our culture is one in which the impulses which fuel stalking behaviour – the conviction that one has the right to become intimate with and gain knowledge about other people, even strangers, and the counter impulse to expose our deepest and darkest desires for all to see – are promoted as an ideal. It is a culture where the laws, customs and traditions that previously governed human interaction are in decline. It is a world, in short, in which the boundary between self and other has become dangerously blurred. In such a culture, stalking becomes an appropriate symptom, perhaps even an inevitable product.

The impulse towards constant visibility and accessibility in celebrity culture means that our understanding of privacy has changed. Ours is a time when the boundaries separating the private and public spheres have never been so blurred. Isn't there something inappropriate about our fascination with celebrities? Isn't there something perverse about our readiness to display our private worlds – our emotions, habits, and desires – openly, publicly, in an endless stream of 'reality' TV programmes? The digital culture into which we are so thoroughly immersed plunges us into a universe of endless 'legitimate' stalking – constantly tracked via our credit card, mobile phone or computer use, subject to harassment by telemarketing and the 'silent' phone call.

In fact, the rise of the internet is itself symptomatic of the way contemporary culture is fuelled by the impulses that typify stalking. As a medium, the internet lends itself to obsessive, voyeuristic behaviour, as it enables one person to observe, survey and control a whole world unobserved. Its very nature encourages the anonymous gathering of information. 'Cyberstalking' at its most harmless is the practice of finding out about an individual using a search engine. It's very easy to find information about a person, perhaps even a photo, using a search engine. It only takes a second to be 'googled'. But, more disturbingly, other search tools are able, as one website puts it, 'to search, gather and report detailed intelligence on almost anyone or anything on the planet.' For as little as $9.99 you can find anybody's e-mail address, or uncover the identity behind an e-mail alias. The internet houses mechanisms for 'tracking' celebrities, such as CelebFanMail.com, which trades in the addresses of the famous, or 'Gawker Stalker', the celebrity-spotting site. A website like findadeath.com, the epitome of our prurient fascination with celebrities, enables users to do things like take a photographic tour of Jill Dando's last journey, viewing the shops she went into and signs she must have seen – as if they are shadowing her, like a stalker.

Of course our apparent freedom to indulge online is checked by a range of counter-stalking devices. Individuals leave uncoverable traces wherever they go, whenever they use a cash machine or buy something with a credit card. The paranoid underside of the internet is the constant threat of being subject to secret surveillance by sinister unknown networks. A myriad of tracking devices – 'data miners', 'adware', 'spyware', 'malware' – can invade your computer, log your surfing patterns and, most maliciously, attempt to steal personal information such as passwords or other data you have stored.

The stealthy convergence of stalking behaviour and culture at large is reason enough, perhaps, to explain why we have come to produce and consume so many films and books about stalking itself. But there are other reasons, too. Stalking is a very real and disturbing phenomenon. In 1998 a report published by the US Department of Justice estimated that 8 per cent of adult women and 2 per cent of adult men had been stalked at some point in their lives.[1] In June 2004, the British Crime Survey announced that in the previous year more than 1.2 million British women and 900,000 men were the victims of stalking.[2] It follows, then, that films and TV shows will attempt to represent a phenomenon that fascinates and scares us in the real world.

Stalking is also an especially dramatic form of behaviour that lends itself to representation in fiction, film and TV. It involves in real life the kind of behaviour which, paradoxically, we imagine would feature only in the movies. Someone breaks into the house of the girl he is obsessed with, steals a photo album, and sends the photos back to her one by one.[3] A man moves into the same building as a woman he won't stop pestering. He leaves books on her doorstep – horror stories like Stephen King's *Nightmares and Dreamscapes* or Dean Koontz's *Mr Murder*. She throws them over a fence only to find them outside her door the next day. Served with a restraining order he then spends months digging a tunnel under her bathroom floor – undetected – so he can enter underneath the vanity unit.[4] These are real cases, but worthy of a Hollywood film pitch.

What's more, stalking behaviour is characterized by a distinctive logic of escalation: it's not a one-off crime, but one in which progressively more serious attacks are repeated over time. This lends itself well to creating narrative suspense. In a film or novel, knowing a stalker is 'out there' means continually waiting on tenterhooks for the next intrusion. This is how the device is used in much stalking fiction, from slasher movies such as *Halloween* (1978), to Gillian Cross's novel for teenagers, *Tightrope* (1999) and the recent storyline featuring 'the stalker' in the Australian soap opera, *Home and Away* (stalking is especially suited to this supremely repetitive genre, which depends upon cliffhangers).

The close match between real stalking cases and stories in literature and film explains why we can find eerily modern portrayals of stalking behaviour in a whole range of novels stretching back over two centuries, and in film from the earliest days of cinema – long before our contemporary 'stalking culture' begins. Seduction stories, Gothic novels, crime fiction, ghost stories and horror films, all commonly feature one person stalking another, whether it is an unrequited lover, as in Dante's *Purgatory* or Dickens's *Bleak House*, or something more monstrous, like Dracula or the *Peer Gynt*-whistling serial killer in the 1931 film *m*. Alternatively, we might see the stalkers who populate contemporary film and fiction as twisted versions of the questing figures who feature in established literary genres, like detective fiction or the love story. One critic says we can find examples of stalking as far back as classic mythology and the Bible.[5] This doesn't mean stalking was conceived of in previous times just as it is in our own, but it does suggest that being shadowed is a fundamental human fear.

If stalking is something that frightens us, then this begs the question: why have we continued to consume books or films about it? Actually, this taps into a much wider debate than just stalking fiction. The puzzle of why we repeat unpleasurable experiences in art has engaged theorists of art and literature since Aristotle. There may be something cathartic about watching stalking films or reading about stalking, in that observing the troubled relationships of others refreshes our sense of what is valuable about our own. Those who are themselves the unfortunate ones may find a small consolation in the reminder that their experience is not unique. But certainly the overall appeal of stalking fiction is like the thrill we gain from crime fiction or horror fiction: we are able to acknowledge, safely, in the comfort of our home or the cinema seat, the frightening things in the world (and with stalking this means the potential for a relationship with another person to spiral out of control), while also indulging in the fantasy that they can be controlled or eliminated, either by socially appointed guardians, like the private detective, or plucky ordinary people, like the 'final girl' in the slasher film.

Following, persecuting, shadowing is so ubiquitous in literature and cinema that we cannot speak of the 'stalking' novel or film as a separate *genre*, i.e. as a set artistic form with narrative conventions that are recognizably the same from example to example, as in, say, detective fiction or sitcom. Nevertheless some basic structures and conventions recur in 'stalking texts', and I'll be referring to these in this book. At its most fundamental, the narrative structure of a stalking text is as follows. One malicious, obsessed, psychopathological, or aggrieved individual persecutes another, innocent, more vulnerable person – someone at least undeserving of such excessive punishment in the eyes of any reasonable person, such as the reader or viewer. Sometimes the aggressor is a stranger but more often someone the victim knows. The persecutor will seem ordinary and innocuous, perhaps even charming, at the start, though certain aspects of their character will alert the reader or viewer (usually before the main character is aware of it) to his or her potential danger. As the story goes on this dark side will become progressively darker and more visible to the victim and surrounding characters. The motivation behind the stalking behaviour is usually connected with the desire to love or to be loved.

This pattern emerges at its purest in Clint Eastwood's 1971 film *Play Misty For Me*, the film which has a good claim to be the first proper stalking film – i.e. one that wasn't simply another obsessive-love story or horror movie, but which distilled all our fears about stalking into a melodramatic, 'slasher'-style plot two decades before we really knew we had them, and which served as a kind of blueprint for later examples of the stalking film, such as *Fatal Attraction* (1987) and *One Hour Photo* (2002). The story is about Dave Garver, played by Eastwood himself, a hip local DJ, about to break into the big time, who encounters in a bar one of the regular callers to his show, Evelyn Draper, a sexy-voiced woman who always asks for the same dreamy jazz song, 'Misty' by Erroll Garner. They agree to have a no-strings-attached one-night-stand, but she begins to persecute him relentlessly, first via phone calls and notes, then by sabotaging his job interview with a major radio company, and eventually by knifing Garver's cleaning woman (who she assumes is a rival) and abducting his girlfriend.

Though the word 'stalking' is never once uttered in the film, stalking is clearly what it depicts to anyone watching the film now. As one website puts it, 'It really is a story you might read about in the paper.'[6]

Why it took until 1971 for stalking to begin to enter the cultural consciousness is a complicated question which the rest of this book will try to explain. But we can draw a general conclusion at this point, and this is that stalking and its representations in films and books reflect a pervasive anxiety in contemporary culture about the blurred boundaries between supposedly normal ways of relating to another person and apparently 'abnormal' ones – especially the boundary between acceptable and unacceptable ways of expressing *love*. Our perception of stalking, as I'll argue in this book, always revolves around the question of what is normal, and this means that it forces us to acknowledge an uncomfortable similarity between ourselves and the figure of the stalker – otherwise too easily dismissed as just another 'weirdo' or 'psycho'. It's not that we are all potential stalkers, nor even that stalking behaviour is a symptom of our increasingly pathological culture. The point is that stalking, to a greater extent than other serious crimes, revolves around desires and emotions we all share. In this respect, the boundary that separates ordinary people like you and I from the dangerous 'other', the stalker figure who appears in numerous films and books, is less secure than we might think.

CHAPTER ONE

What is Stalking?

Stalker: [3.] b. A person who pursues another, esp. as part of an investigation
or with criminal intent; *spec.* one who follows or harasses someone (often a
public figure) with whom he or she has become obsessed.
Oxford English Dictionary

Stalking, in the sense of systematic harassment, was formally defined only
recently. The above entry appeared in the *Oxford English Dictionary* in 1997,
following media interest in the phenomenon over the previous decade.
Stalking is defined by forensic psychologists, those who have done most
research into the phenomenon, as 'a constellation of behaviours in which one
individual inflicts on another repeated unwanted intrusions and communications'.[1] More precise definitions are difficult to produce because stalking
doesn't come down to a single act. It involves a multitude of acts – not all of
which are illegal in themselves (an obscene phone call is, sending an e-mail
or standing outside a house is not). Nevertheless, as the authors of a recent
study say, 'As far as the general public is concerned, it may be that stalking
is like great art: they cannot define it, but they know it when they see it'.[2]

For stalking is a term that has come to feature more and more in every-day use. It is a byword for acting 'weird', for showing an unhealthy fascination with someone or something, an alternative for 'freaky' or 'creepy'. It is often used as an insult. We use it ironically if we keep bumping into someone: 'I'm not stalking you!' But it is also quite common now to find the word used in a more positive sense on the internet, in chat rooms or on 'blogs', in the context of being a fan – when someone discovers the work of a novelist or musician and decides to 'stalk' the rest of his work, for example. Common to all these definitions is a sense that to stalk is to act obsessively, in excess of what would be considered 'proper' or 'normal' behaviour.

Of course the term stalking is not a 1990s neologism. The roots of the term 'to stalk' come from the frequentative form of the Old English word '-*stealcian*', as in *bestealcian* 'to steal along'. Just as 'to talk' is 'to tell frequently', so to stalk is repeatedly to 'steal along'. The way the term is used now to denote 'harassment' is therefore a metaphor: we imagine one person perse-cuting another in the way a hunter patiently but purposefully tracks an animal he is going to kill and use for food or clothing.

For centuries the term was applied almost exclusively to the stealthy tracking movement of animals, especially predatory ones such as big cats, or the hunting of them by other animals or humans. This sense still exists – as a glance at the other sections of the stalking definition in the *OED* will confirm. You can still go on 'deer stalking' holidays in Scotland, or buy from the 'Stalker' range of hunting-style clothing by the US company L. L. Bean. Interestingly, though, the term's associations with hunting carried connota-tions of criminality or terror from the outset.

A stalker was defined in 1424 as 'one who stalks game illegally, a poacher' and in 1508 as 'one who prowls about for purposes of theft'. Stalking was often a term applied to ghosts, as in Shakespeare's *Hamlet* (Act 1, Scene 1) or the first line of Karl Marx's *The Communist Manifesto* ('A spectre is stalking Europe . . .'). Gradually, throughout the Nineteenth and Twentieth Centuries uses of the term 'to stalk' began to encompass the hunting of one human being by another. In William Thackeray's 1855 novel *The Newcomes: Memoirs of a Most Respectable Family*, for example, there is the line 'As he was pursuing the deer, she stalked his lordship'. Arthur Ransome's 1947 'Swallows and Amazons' adventure story for children, *Great Northern?*, contains the exchange: '"We must just go on, pretending we don't know we're being stalked . . ." "And then the stalker will get a bit careless and let himself be seen," said Roger.'[3]

The old and new senses of the word – hunting animals and harassing other people – are not divorced, then. Hunting has always been associated with a particular image of masculinity. One of the chapters in Baden Powell's famous manual for the Scouting Movement, *Scouting for Boys*, published in 1908, is on 'Stalking', teaching boys how to track animals. The instructions reflect an image of the hunter as lone killer, a disciplined and silent assassin. In fact, the stalkers we read about nowadays *are* malicious hunters, their victims prey, though they are far from the glorified image evoked in books like *Scouting for Boys*. The connotation is frequently invoked in the discourse surrounding serial killers. In Thomas Harris's novel *The Silence of the Lambs*, for example, the serial killer at large has been given the name 'Buffalo Bill' by the tabloids because he skins his victims. He perceives of his grisly practice in hunting terms (e.g. 'he didn't want to field-dress her here'[4]).

But unlike hunting, stalking as we understand it now is not limited to one particular location or time-frame, nor one method of pursuit. Stalking involves repeated, persistent, unsolicited communications or physical approaches to the victim. It can involve letters, telephone calls, text messages, e-mails and other signs that the stalker has visited (like damage to a victim's car). A stalker may literally follow the victim, or keep watch on his or her house. Stalking also encompasses more indirect forms of persecution such as ordering products or sending unsolicited mail on the victim's behalf or instigating spurious legal actions. The result of such behaviour is to induce in the victim a state of alarm and distress or fear of physical violence. These fears are reasonable, for stalking very often results in violence to a person or their property.

It was in the 1970s that the term stalking began to shift more decisively from referring to the hunting of animals to the persecution of human beings. This decade sees the term used in American newspapers in relation to two forms of 'hunting': first, the pursuit of celebrities, initially by photographers and then by deranged men, and second, serial killing.

In the early 1960s a new kind of photo-journalist had been identified: the *paparazzo* (the name derived from a character in Federico Fellini's 1960 portrayal of the emptiness of celebrity culture, *La Dolce Vita*) whose job is to pursue celebrities and get shots of them engaged in private and public business. The *paparazzi* were first defined in a *Time* magazine article of 14 April 1961, which described them as 'a ravenous wolf pack of freelance photographers who *stalk* big names for a living and fire with flash guns at point-blank range'.[5] The article portrays celebrity pursuit as an activity far removed from idolization. It depicts the photographers as menacing harassers who are openly hostile about their subjects, hell bent on catching them in 'trouble' or provoking them into causing it themselves. The language is the language of hunting: celebrities are the prey, divided into 'big' or 'small' game.

Tales of paparazzi excess are now legion in celebrity culture. The *Time* article gives the example of one 'paparazzo', Tazio Secchiaroli, who, having been 'called a dirty name' by the movie star Ava Gardner, 'vengefully hid for hours in a cardboard box on a Cinecitta movie lot, [then] finally got what he came for: an unflattering shot of Ava in an old bath towel, hair wet and stringy as a mop'.[6] Perhaps the most disturbing example of the paparazzo-as-stalker is Ted Leyson's relentless pursuit of the famously reclusive Greta Garbo. The series of photographs Leyson took on her 84th birthday in 1989 are truly disturbing, for what is on display is not so much a trophy celebrity, but an act of violent intrusion into the life of an old woman who had withdrawn from the public eye 48 years before, fear in her eyes as she is cornered in her limousine. A week after they were taken Garbo died.

Photo-journalism naturally absorbs the traditional hunting connotations of the term stalking. The stalking capacity of the reporter is fuelled by the inherent intrusive potential of the camera. The camera 'shoots', it *takes* (i.e. steals) pictures. In an essay on photography which first appeared in *The New York Review of Books* in the mid 1970s, Susan Sontag describes the touring photographer as 'an armed version of the solitary walker reconnoitering, stalking, cruising the urban inferno, the voyeuristic stroller who discovers the city as a landscape of voluptuous extremes'.[7] By the late 1970s, the verb stalking was commonly used for such work. A *Newsweek* article of 12 September 1977 describes a photographer, Ron Galella, as having 'made a career of stalking [Jackie Kennedy] with a camera until she went to court to keep him at a distance'.[8]

It would be a mistake to overstate the links between photography and serial murder, but there is a similar general logic at work in both, which revolves around the 'capturing' of a targeted individual (often for the image they represent) and involves a similar dynamic of power and control. Serial killers are not stalkers per se, as stalking involves someone known in some way to the stalker, while serial-killing was, significantly, previously known as 'stranger-killing'. But serial killers typically stalk their victims in some way before attacking them. In his 6-point breakdown of the different stages of serial killing, Joel Norris terms number 3 'The Trolling Phase', when the killer searches for a victim ('trolling' is a kind of sauntering or cruising).[9]

The media took to referring to the 'Son of Sam', the gunman who terrorized New York in the summer of 1977, as a 'stalker': he was described as having 'stalked his prey', having a 'favorite stalking ground', and indulging in 'night-stalking'.[10] Subseqently stalking was a label frequently used in newspaper reports of serial-killings and rapes, and also in reviews of slasher movies like *Halloween* (1978) or horror films like *The Shining* (1980). Another serial killer, Richard Ramirez, who murdered 12 people in a period from June 1984 to August 1985, was dubbed the 'Night Stalker' by Los Angeles media.

The use of the term stalking and its variants in these two spheres paved the way for the proper entry into the language of the term stalking in its contemporary sense in the late 1980s and early 1990s. At this time it was applied to a kind of composite version of the two modern hunters we have just been considering, the hostile paparazzo and the psychopathological serial murderer – specifically, a man person (usually a man) who becomes obsessed by a celebrity and ends up attacking him or her.

If we had to pinpoint one moment when modern 'stalking culture' began, it would be the murder of the TV actress Rebecca Schaeffer by one Robert John Bardo in 1989. Bardo was an intense, intelligent young man (though a teacher once described him as 'a time bomb on the verge of exploding'). Schaeffer wrote back to him, saying his letter was 'the most beautiful' she had ever received. She finished with a sketch of a peace sign and a love heart, and signed it 'with love from Rebecca'. On receiving it Bardo wrote in his diary: 'When I think of her, I would like to become famous to impress her'. He had over 100 videotapes featuring the actress. He later explained that she 'came into my life in the right moment. She was brilliant, pretty, outrageous, her innocence impressed me. She turned into a goddess for me, an idol. Since then, I turned an atheist, I only adored her.'[11]

In 1987 he twice attempted to enter Burbank studios, where she was filming the TV show *My Sister Sam*, the second time with a knife concealed in his jacket. After being refused entry he wrote in his diary: 'I don't lose. Period.' Then he saw her film *Class Struggle in Beverly Hills*, in which Schaeffer's character was shown in bed with an actor. Bardo was appalled. This proved, he thought, that Schaeffer had become 'one more of the bitches of Hollywood' and ought to be punished for her loose morals. He sketched a diagram of her body, marking the points where he planned to shoot her, and asked his brother to buy him a gun.

He then found Schaeffer's address through the Division of Motor Vehicles, and travelled to LA with the gun and a copy of J. D. Salinger's novel *The Catcher in the Rye*. On 17 July 1989, he knocked on her door and introduced himself as her biggest fan. She thanked him before politely dismissing him. He went to have breakfast. He returned an hour later and shot her, point blank, on the doorstep.

Bardo was by no means the first man to stalk and attack a celebrity. Schaeffer's murder followed on from other high-profile stalking cases involving public figures: Mark Chapman's murder of John Lennon in December 1980, John Hinckley's attempt to assassinate President Reagan in March 1981 to impress Jodie Foster, the stabbing of actress Teresa Saldana by Arthur Jackson in 1982, and Margaret Ray's non-violent harassment of TV talkshow host David Letterman in 1988–9. But what was different about the Bardo case was that it quickly led to a vast proliferation of material – in newspapers and other media, as well as academic and clinical literature – that sought to link these events and to define the perpetrators as symptomatic of a distinctive phenomenon. Newspapers cited as damning evidence, for example, the fact that Bardo possessed a copy of *The Catcher in the Rye*, because this book was central to the deluded motivation behind Chapman's murder of Lennon. A newspaper article published on 17 February 1992 called 'In The Mind of the Stalker' described Bardo as 'a symbol of a spreading national menace' and 'an archetypal stalker'.[12]

It is difficult to believe now, but contemporary accounts of previous attacks on celebrities do not describe them as 'stalking' stories. Analyses of the murder of John Lennon in widely circulated news magazines like *Life* or *Newsweek*, for example, never use the term, even though it has some of the key ingredients of what came to be seen as the 'classic' stalker case, featuring a loner with an identity crisis and an unhealthy obsession with a celebrity.[13] But after Schaeffer's murder, the term 'stalker' was here to stay. Not only was it the accepted term in the media, it also became inscribed in the law. In their response to her death, the Los Angeles Police Department established its Threat Management Unit, aimed at dealing with stalking cases in the light of increasing psychological research about the phenomenon. In 1990, the state of California passed the first anti-stalking law. Stalking had become an officially designated crime.

By 1992, 30 more states had joined California, and all US states had passed such laws by 1993. This was followed in 1996 by a federal, interstate anti-stalking law designed to cover stalkers who cross the boundaries between US states. In 1997 a similar law was introduced in Britain, 'The Protection from Harassment Act', designed to 'to make provision for protecting persons from harassment and similar conduct'. By 2000 many other countries had followed suit: Australia, Canada, Japan, and most countries in Western Europe.

The reason for such an explosion of anti-stalking legislation was the recognition, as more media coverage was given to stalking and more academic research was undertaken, that stalking was not just a crime perpetrated on celebrities. Rather the pattern of obsession and persecution involved in celebrity stalking was also played out on a daily basis amongst 'ordinary' people. Everyday cases of stalking began to be a staple of newspaper articles in the late 1980s and early 1990s. The availability of anti-stalking laws meant that there was an inexhaustible supply of stalking cases dealt with in the courts, which could then be the focus of media reports.

What happened as a result of Bardo's stalking of Schaeffer was that stalking began to be the subject of a 'moral panic'. The 'moral panic' is a sociological category, first defined by Stanley Cohen in his 1972 book *Folk Devils and Moral Panics,* which denotes an 'episode, condition, person or group of persons' that have irrationally been regarded as an extreme 'threat to societal values and interests'.[14] A related concept used by criminologists is the 'crime panic' where the public come to believe, mainly because of media dramatization, that a particular crime is more prevalent and threatening than it is.

It is not that such panics are *purely* hysterical (i.e. imaginary) but that they focus disproportionately on just one issue amongst many which may be perceived as a threat to the prevailing social order. Recent examples in Britain would include the panics about paedophilia or child abduction, or the taking of the drug 'ecstasy'. A set of circumstances builds up into a vortex of cultural debate and representation. The opinions of 'moral guardians' such as politicians, religious leaders, cultural commentators and experts are enlisted. Films and TV programmes keep the problem visible and deepen concern. Methods of dealing with the problem are developed by the police and health professionals.

A moral panic will gradually subside as public consciousness becomes focused elsewhere, though it continues to be part of cultural memory. But some moral or crime panics result in significant changes to legal or social policy. Stalking is clearly one such example. For even though we are no longer in the grip of a *panic* about stalking, now, in the early twenty-first century, stalking is neverthless firmly part of the fabric of our society, given its inscription in the law.

Legal and Psychological Definitions

Because use of the label 'stalking' by forensic psychologists and psychiatrists begins in the 1990s, it doesn't mean they were uninterested in the phenomenon before then. In the 1970s and 1980s there were important studies of 'sexual harassment', particularly of women (who had received obscene phone calls, or been physically pursued, etc.).[15] In the 1980s there was a focus on considering erotomania or sexual harassment specifically within a criminological context.[16] Nevertheless, it was only following the high-profile celebrity-stalking cases of the late 1980s, such as Robert Bardo's, that there was a sustained effort to produce a system of classification which could help in the prosecution and/or psychiatric treatment of offenders.

Stalking is often associated by psychiatrists and psychologists with specific mental disorders, especially pathological narcissism. Yet there is no one disorder or syndrome that can explain it. Psychologists therefore stress that stalking is a *behaviour*. It is not necessarily abnormal to have an unhealthy obsession with somebody. It is when this obsession is *acted upon*, however, that unacceptable consequences may ensue. This emphasis on behaviour rather than state of mind is also useful from a legal perspective: it is not a crime to think in a certain way but it is a crime to act upon certain thoughts. While this removes some of the problems from diagnosing or prosecuting stalking, it is still not so simple. For there is still the question about *which* behaviour actually counts as stalking. Is it following someone? Phoning or texting someone? Writing a letter to someone? Standing outside someone's house? Most would agree that it is the way a perpetrator may go about these activities that is important here, and also their frequency. Sending a person an unsolicited text message telling them that you can't stop thinking about them is one matter, adding that if they don't respond you will kill them is quite another. Sending several messages is another matter still. Standing outside a person's home is not illegal, but if someone does so while holding a knife in his hand, it clearly becomes threatening.

Surveying the different anti-stalking laws in operation throughout the United States reveals four consistent elements in their definition of what stalking entails:

1. Stalking involves a 'course of conduct' – that is, actions (e.g. harassment by letter, phone or e-mail) repeated over time, not a single event. Most states consider a course of conduct to include two or more incidents.

2. Stalking violates an individual's personal right to privacy. Even though stalking occurs in what we might think of as public spaces (restaurants, bars, etc., even online) it is assumed by us law that the individual has a right to privacy in them.

3. There must be evidence of a threat and/or fear having been caused. This is measurable by an appeal to a 'reasonable person'. If such a person would consider the course of conduct frightening then it is likely to be considered stalking.

4. The stalking does not have to be directed towards the target of communications but can involve threatening or implying a threat against associates, friends, family, pets, or property.

The British 'Protection from Harassment Act' runs along similar lines. It is designed to protect against two related things: harassment, which it defines as 'causing the person alarm or distress', and 'putting people in fear of violence'. Like the American legislation it looks for a 'course of conduct', which it defines as causing another to fear that violence will be used against him or her on 'at least two occasions'. The British law emphasizes the fact that the accused 'knows or ought to know' that his actions are likely to amount to harassment or to cause fear of violence. Again it tests this by imagining whether 'a reasonable person in possession of the same information would think the course of conduct amounted to harassment of the other'.

Overall, then, legal and psychological approaches are careful to define stalking as something you *do* rather than something that defines who you *are*. There is no such thing as an 'identikit' profile of the stalker – despite the impression given in much popular fiction and film. Ben Elton's stalker-thriller *Blast from the Past* (1999), for example, sees its villain casually defined as 'a most specific pervert'.[17] Stalking is not a sexual perversion. Nevertheless, classifying the different kinds of stalking case is deemed crucial by those who need to prevent stalking, prosecute those accused of it, or treat those who have been convicted. The way forensic psychologists have chosen to come up with a valid 'typology of stalking cases' has therefore been determined by an emphasis on actions rather than identities. What is considered important are the motivations behind a case of stalking and the desires it is intended to satisfy. Drawing on some of the most cited studies,[18] we could summarize this typology using the following three categories.

Former-intimate stalking. The majority of stalking cases involve perpetrators and victims who are 'former intimates', as they have had an intimate relationship that has now ended. Former-intimate stalking cases can be divided into three main kinds. Most common is when one individual (usually a woman) breaks off a relationship and the rejected party (usually a man) begins to harass them to force them to change their mind or to punish them. Such cases may be the result of a long-term relationship, such as a marriage, or simply the outcome of a brief affair. The break-up may be the result of abuse, but may equally be because one person simply decides the two people are incompatible or the relationship has run its course.

Former-intimate stalking also occurs in the workplace, when one employee persecutes the person – usually a superior – they think has caused them to be suspended or dismissed, or when one employee tries to begin an intimate relationship with another but feels rejected. The third kind of relationship in this category involves people who have had a previous professional relationship with someone that is now ended. Curiously, it is this kind of former intimate stalking which has produced a kind of sub-genre in stalking literature, the memoir about being stalked. The psychiatrist Doreen Orion wrote in her memoir *I Know You Really Love Me* about being persecuted by a former patient, while two British lecturers, Robert Fine and Gregory Dart, have recently published autobiographical accounts of being stalked by one of their students.[19]

The motives behind former-intimate stalking are always either a) to try to change the mind of the victim or b) to teach them a lesson. This kind of relationship is likely to be more violent that the other kind of stalking relationships because the offender and the victim know each other. These are also the cases of the shortest duration.

Desired-intimate stalking. These cases differ most obviously from the previous category because they involve people who did not have a previous relationship. In fact, the only relationship between stalker and victim *is* the stalking process. This brings in a distinctive 'self-fulfilling' logic typical of stalking: the desire to form one kind of relationship results in the formation of a different kind of relationship. Desired-intimate stalking is motivated by the desire on the part of the stalker to gain some kind of recognition from the target. Typical of this kind of relationship is an exceedingly prolonged programme of harassment. Typically the stalker will write letters (or communicate in other ways) to the love object telling them how much s/he desires them, believing mistakenly that the declaration of love will result in the object returning their affection. As time passes and there is no positive response, the attention will become persecutory, perhaps resulting in confrontation.

This category would include the many cases of celebrity stalking. But it also occurs in everyday life, when one person becomes obsessed with someone they have met or seen in an non-intimate and apparently (to the victim) innocuous way. Also included in this group would be those some psychiatrists term 'incompetents'. These are people who intend to court someone they desire, but who are ignorant of or indifferent to the conventions of courting. As a result, their advances are off-putting or even terrifying. Unlike former-intimate stalking, desired-intimate cases involve at least some degree of *delusion* about the true nature of the stalker's relationship with the desired person.

Many stalkers in this kind of relationship are said to suffer from schizophrenia or bipolar disorder (manic depression). They are likely to be socially impaired without any experience of meaningful intimate relationships. At the less extreme end of the scale, desired-intimate stalking behaviour fulfils a need for intimacy and closeness, linked to fantasies that stalker and victim will eventually end up in a loving relationship. But at its worst, this category includes 'erotomaniacs'. Where many intimacy seekers have the mistaken belief that the love object may be *persuaded* to return their feelings, erotomania is distinguished by an erroneous conviction on the part of the sufferer that the object of their desire actually loves them in return. Because this involves a full-blown delusional disorder, these cases last for a long time and are very difficult to prevent. Given the nature of delusion, the deluded person cannot simply be persuaded to accept 'reality'. Even intense therapy is not guaranteed to work.

Desired-intimate stalking is the only category of stalking mainly to be constituted by female stalkers. Usually the object of their attention is an older male, who occupies a more elevated socio-economic position. Desired-intimate stalkers are considered less likely to seek to physically harm their victim than former intimates.

Non-intimate persecution. The first two categories both deal essentially with intimate relationships: former-intimate stalking is where a close relationship has broken down, while desired-intimacy stalking seeks to establish one or mistakenly believes one exists. The third category includes stalking cases that have nothing to do with the desire for a close relationship. The motivation is to punish another person for a perceived insult or injury, real or imagined, something that has in some way wounded the stalker's sense of self.

This category includes people known to the victim, someone who feels another has done them an injustice in the workplace, say, or damaged their reputation amongst friends. The stalker seeks by his (or her) persecution not simply to gain revenge but to achieve *vindication*. But this category also includes persecution by those unknown to the target. At its most dangerous, this means sociopathic stalking, as in the cases of serial killers, rapists, or the kind of people referred to more generally by clinicians as 'predatory' stalkers, those who 'pursue their desires for sexual gratification and control. The stalking is a rehearsal for the stalker's violent sexual fantasies and a partial satisfaction of voyeuristic and sadistic desires'.[20]

The 'Narcissistic Linking Fantasy'

We know what kinds of stalking case are most common, and the kinds of people who are most likely to become stalkers. But it's not so easy to say what actually turns feelings of rage, frustration, inadequacy, even love, into stalking. After all, if one was seeking an outlet to express overwhelming emotions, one could turn to numerous forms of anti-social or criminal behaviour. Why stalking?

The best way of answering this question is to turn to psychoanalysis, in particular its understanding of how three fundamental psychic phenomena inter-relate: 'desire', 'fantasy' and 'symptom'. Desires do not exist within us, fully formed, waiting to be let out, but require something to pull them into shape, to give them a form – much as cinematic *mise-en-scène* transforms a basic screenplay into a film. This element is fantasy. Fantasy should not be mistaken as a synonym for 'whimsy' or 'escapism', as something that will evaporate when confronted with 'the truth'. Rather, it is the very 'support' for our experience of reality. Fantasy functions as a 'frame' through which we perceive ourselves and the world around us.

If fantasy is what 'stages' desire, then a symptom – the outward manifestation of a psychic disorder – is what stages fantasy, in turn. To use an example given by the psychoanalysts Laplanche and Pontalis, the symptom of agrophobia might be the pathological expression of a fantasy of prostitution, or street-walking.[21] In the case of stalking, the underlying desire is to be loved or accepted, the fantasy is of an intimate relationship with the person who might function as the object of this desire – one which usually modulates into a fantasy of revenge or punishment, once the possibility of the desired relationship is closed off – and the symptom is the actual stalking, the compulsive pattern of escalating behaviour.

The importance of intimacy in psychological and psychoanalytic explanations of stalking underlines the fact that, at its most basic, stalking is rooted in a problematic experience of relationships. It is the result of one person's inability to accept the reality about a relationship with another, the fact that the person they are preoccupied by does not wish, or no longer wishes, to have a relationship with them – or, at least, not the same kind of relationship. Stalkers are unable to understand or accept the conventional social signals that structure relationships. In the wrong kind of individual, the refusal to accept the reality about a relationship results in a symptomatic 'acting out' – an escalation of intrusions into the life of the other, with violence as a potential outcome.

One of the four suicidal characters in Nick Hornby's 2005 novel *A Long Way Down*, the teenager Jess, indignantly denies accusations that she stalked her ex-boyfriend, Chas:

I didn't think it was stalking when someone owed you an explanation. Being owed an explanation is like being owed money, and not just a fiver, either. Five or six hundred quid minimum, more like. If you were owed five or six hundred quid minimum and the person who owed it to you was avoiding you, then you're bound to knock on his door late at night, when you know he's going to be in. People get serious about that sort of money. They call in debt collectors, and break people's legs, but I never went that far. I showed some restraint.[22]

This articulates clearly the logic many stalkers subscribe to. The stalker feels a sense of injustice, a conviction that he or she has given another person something or done something for them that has not been reciprocated. In some cases, this may be something quite specific: someone might harass another over a real or perceived broken promise. Occasionally, it might be the result of a delusion, as in the case of Kenneth Gause's stalking of chat-show host Johnny Carson in the 1990s – because he was convinced Carson owed him $6 million – but more often the debt is less easy to determine. Jess says she seeks an explanation, but what would this explanation have achieved? Trying to explain yourself to your stalker is often the worse thing you can do. All it does is prolong the relationship and feeds the fantasies or rage of the stalker by providing new material. The British Network for Surviving Stalking advises victims not to agree to a stalker's requests to meet, as 'all that will happen is they will be in your company and feeding their "problem"'.[23]

Stalking is an extreme way of reminding its victim that they are in a *relationship* with another person. It is impossible not to be part of this relationship, for whatever you do in response to what the stalker says or does – even if it is to avoid responding – still constitutes a form of response. The act of stalking traps the victim in the 'game'. This is one reason why, compared with other crimes, stalking cases are inordinately prolonged. Stalkers never give up. Even after being sentenced and imprisoned, and confronted with the outcomes of their actions, many still persist with their harassment. Stalking ensures that the other person cannot stay outside of the relationship. As Gregory Dart puts it in his own account of being stalked, 'it was clear that I had become trapped in a relationship in which there seemed no way of not being involved'.[24]

It is an irony typical of stalking that what is produced by the original failure for a normal relationship to develop is a relationship of a more intense kind between stalker and victim, as the person who is stalked is unable to escape the stalker. The two become yoked together in a mirrored pattern of behaviour, both preoccupied, in different ways and for different reasons, with each other. A common feature of real-life stalking cases is the stalker, rather ironically, accusing the victim of being obsessed with him or her. The process of mirroring is expressed perhaps most powerfully in Ian McEwan's fictional account of stalking, *Enduring Love* (1998). The narrator, science journalist Joe Rose, settles into a routine with his stalker, Jed Parry, which would be comic if it wasn't for the overall sense of foreboding conveyed by Parry's obsession. Each day Rose stares out of his window to catch a glimpse of Parry coming to stand outside his house. If he leaves the building, Parry follows him, before turning down a side street. Parry reads all of Rose's published articles, looking for hidden messages. Rose reads about de Clérambault's syndrome, the disorder from which Parry suffers, hoping for clues which can help him explain and predict the painful course of events. The dark irony is that both men – one deluded, the other innocent – have become mirror-images of each other, both watching each other, both reading voraciously about each other.

Stalking is a drastically literal method of getting another person to become just like the stalker. In other words, it is, fundamentally, a *narcissistic* disorder and crime, because its central feature is the collapse of a stable boundary between self and other. To put it more psychoanalytically, there is a disturbance in the relationship between subject and object – where 'object' is understood in a specialized sense as something outside the self, which we latch onto unconsciously in order to procure satisfaction. The object can either be a thing or a person.

The fact is that, from a psychoanalytic perspective, narcissism is a 'normal' part of our psychological make-up, because the libidinal investment in one's own self is a necessary precondition of learning to love others.[25] But psychiatrists and forensic psychologists have identified a whole range of narcissistic pathologies, from temporary reactions to full blown 'Narcissistic Personality Disorder'(NPD), which make it easier to understand the way stalking works.

'NPD' is what is known as a 'borderline' state. It is a condition on the borderline between neurosis and psychosis, and which is characterized not via conventional clear *symptoms* (as are found in disorders such as obsessional neurosis or schizophrenia) but more vague *dissatisfactions*. Borderline cases, according to psychiatrists and psychoanalysts, have become, since the mid-twentieth century, increasingly common in the treatment room.

The main characteristics of the narcissistic personality are grandiosity, extreme self-centredness, and a contradictory lack of interest in and empathy for others and eagerness to receive admiration and approval. But the grandiosity of narcissism originates in what is in fact a weak, fragile sense of self. Narcissistic personalities are particularly prone to idealization of others. They tend to admire someone they regard as outstanding, and 'experience themselves as part of that outstanding person'.[26] The narcissist is unable to *identify with* other people in the proper sense – i.e. use someone as an ideal upon whom to model their behaviour – but tends to regard them as extensions of his or her self.

When another individual is regarded as nothing less than a part of yourself, it is likely to be taken very personally if that person is perceived as rejecting you or to letting you down in some way. When this happens narcissists 'experience immediate hatred and fear, and react by devaluing the former idol'.[27] Hatred comes easily precisely because the narcissistic predisposition to admire another springs ultimately from a deep-rooted sense of inadequacy. It is all too easy for an exalted person to remind the narcissist of their insignificance.

Taking the condition of narcissistic pathology as the starting point, the psychologist J. Reid Meloy has developed a sequential model, based on clinical experience, which shows how stalking behaviour develops in certain individuals. Stalking behaviour, he says, typically proceeds through six different stages, each of which involves feelings or actions that lead logically on to the next:

1. Existence of 'narcissistic linking fantasy'
2. Acute or chronic rejection by desired object
3. Feelings of shame/humiliation
4. Rage-fuelled defence against these feelings
5. 'Behavioural pursuit', intended to hurt, control, damage, or destroy previously desired object
6. Restoration of narcissistic linking fantasy

Stalking begins with the subject creating what Meloy calls a 'narcissistic linking fantasy' in his mind. 'Such fantasies', he says, 'are characterized by conscious thoughts of being loved by or loving, admired by or admiring (idealizing), being exactly like (mirroring) or complementing (twinship), or sharing a destiny with a particular object or person (merger)'.[28] Meloy stresses that such fantasies are not pathological, any more than narcissism itself is abnormal. In fact they are typical of the kinds of attachment everyone forms with another person, from someone we fall in love with to someone we look up to (say a colleague), or a celebrity or public figure whose work or image we value.

Nor is the *outcome* of the narcissistic linking fantasy pathological. It is natural to act upon one's feeling of attachment by making an approach of some sort – e.g. asking someone out for a drink, making a suggestive comment, sending an admiring letter or turning up at a public appearance.

Stage 2 in Meloy's sequence is when the object of one's desire rejects this approach – either acutely (say, crushingly) or repeatedly. This, too, is perfectly normal. We have all suffered rejection by someone we desire. Perhaps we have been turned away by someone we admire. Most of us do not become stalkers as a result. After the rejection, normal people, Meloy says, will 'withdraw' as the object of pursuit has now become aversive. They may feel extreme disappointment or anger, even shame or humiliation, yet their ability to interact socially in other areas of their lives remains intact. If spurned by a potential lover, they will in time turn their attention to another. If rejected by a celebrity or public figure, they may rationalize the failure to reciprocate or perhaps 'de-idealize' this person in their mind, feeling as a result of the rejection that perhaps they weren't that special after all.

It is at the third point in Meloy's sequence that the stalker fails to act as a normal person would. This is because of the impact of the unconscious feeling that a part of him (or herself) has turned against him (or her). Given the tendency of narcissists to perceive of others as 'part objects' whose function is to gratify him/her, they feel 'extraordinarily sensitive to rejection and the feelings of shame or humiliation that accompany it'.[29] To deal with these unbearable feelings, the stalker defends himself with rage (stage 4). This is what leads to the range of behaviours we recognize as stalking (stage 5), as the stalker now attempts to devalue the previously idealized object by hurting, controlling, damaging or even destroying him or her.

Stalking is thus explained by Meloy as the defence mechanism of the pathological narcissistic personality, a way of dominating an object that promised to gratify the stalker but instead has hurt and shamed him or her. This pattern is particularly obvious in celebrity stalking cases, where the initial idealization is replaced by a violently expressed disgust at the victim's 'betrayal'. Men who stalk famous women often express outrage at the apparent infidelity of the desired object. Having seen Schaeffer playing a woman in bed with her lover in one scene in the film *Scenes from the Class Struggle in Beverly Hills*, Robert Bardo told his sister that he aimed to stop the actress from 'forsaking her innocent childlike image for that of an adult fornicating screen whore'.

The sixth stage in Meloy's sequence underlines the powerful grip stalking has on its victims, because it provides the perpetrator with an exquisite kind of satisfaction (though it would be misleading to say it gives the stalker 'pleasure', pure and simple). If the object is sufficiently devalued, he argues, the original 'narcissistic linking fantasy' is restored. What has happened throughout the first five stages is that an ideal or fantasy object has been replaced by the *real* object. The fantasy has thus been shattered. But because of the programme of harassment visited on this real object it is eliminated and replaced once again by an ideal or fantasy version. There is thus a disturbing circularity to stalking behaviour, according to Meloy's model. It suggests why a stalking case is so lengthy and relentless, because the stalker is so determined to restore his internal equilibrium. It also means that simply because a course of stalking conduct has begun, a victory of sorts will inevitably result for the stalker. He or she will have achieved – albeit in a radically different way – the original objective of being linked to his or her object of desire. Clinical experience here runs in tandem with the paradoxical logic which is brought out in many films and books – such as McEwan's *Enduring Love* – which revolve around stalking: the impossibility of a normal relationship results in the establishment of an abnormal relationship.

To see this at work, Meloy gives the example of John Hinckley Jr's stalking of Jodie Foster in the early 1980s. Hinckley (who was diagnosed with narcissistic personality disorder in 1997) has ensured that he will always be linked in our minds with Foster. As Meloy says '[h]er consciousness of him validates his narcissistic linking fantasy, one that perhaps remains a hidden preoccupation for him 17 years later'.[30] After being convicted for his attempted assassination of President Reagan (a bizarre effort to win Foster over) Hinckley wrote a letter to *Time* magazine re-asserting his feelings for her: 'The most important thing in my life is Jodie Foster's love and admiration. If I can't have them, neither can anyone else. We are a historical couple, like Napoleon and Josephine, and a romantic couple like Romeo and Juliet.' Similarly, in the Madonna stalking trial, newspapers jokingly referred to the stalker, Robert Hoskins, as 'Mr Madonna', as one of his threats was dressed up as a marriage proposal, and he had told people he was her husband. Once convicted, fellow inmates called him 'The Material Guy'.

The Victims of Stalking

Stalking has similarities with other crimes, such as serial killing and prowling. But in other ways it is a very unusual crime. Usually what makes something a crime is that it involves an act or series of acts that obviously contravenes a law – e.g. kidnap, murder, fraud, breaking and entering. Though these crimes have victims, how they are affected, or whether they testify, are irrelevant for the actions of the offender to be seen as criminal. Stalking, by contrast, is 'victim-defined' crime. It is not what the offender does, but the effect of his or her actions on the victim that makes it a crime. And the disturbing fact about stalking is that, unlike other crimes, almost anyone – no matter their age, gender, marital status, sexuality, social or cultural background, physical appearance – can find themselves the victim of a stalker (though it's true that there's an especially high incidence amongst celebrities). Nor is it just the main target of the stalker's actions who suffers, but their friends and family do too – sometimes directly, with attacks upon them, or through more indirect means, such as the passing on of sensitive information, or because of the difficulty of dealing with the victim's distress.

With most serious crime, victims end up having to deal with one specific traumatic event, such as an intrusion into their private property or an assault on their person. But because stalking, by its very nature, is a crime that involves persistent and repeated actions – which may be repetitive but often occur irrationally, without warning – it means that the stalking victim suffers from a different kind of trauma, a protracted and repeated one. They don't just have to come to terms with one particular distressing event, but must do this *and* prepare themselves for the next one too. Thus the stalking victim lives in a state of permanent fear, always expecting the worse, regardless of whether an actual threat has been made. Their world – its public and private spaces – seems to have changed, and has become a place full of potential menace. Moreover, it seems that the victim's capacity to exert a reasonable level of control upon this world has diminished as a result of their experience. The loss of control means that, besides obvious alterations in their everyday lives, such as weight loss or the inability to sleep, psychologists report that stalking victims tend to suffer from more long-term 'chronic stress' symptoms, such as the reduced ability to function normally and an excess of 'morbid' thoughts.

What happens when someone is stalked is that there is a radical disturbance in their sense of identity. A consistent sense of self is something most of us have built up as we grow into adulthood. We know, or think we know, our strengths and weaknesses, how we react in certain situations, how others perceive us. But being stalked forces a person to reassess all of this. There is another unpleasant irony here: just as the stalker is often the product of a narcissistic pathology, so his actions ensure that his victim becomes more self-conscious than ever before. He or she naturally becomes more sensitive, often more aggressive, even paranoid. This is something again portrayed accurately by *Enduring Love*. To try and catch Parry making a threat, which would enable the police to take action, Rose takes to secreting a dictating machine in his pocket and wearing a microphone under the lapel of his jacket. But faced with Parry's unshakeable counter-story of the truth behind their encounters, Rose begins to wonder if *he* is the one who's deluded? Is he overdramatizing what is happening to him? Might he actually be *hallucinating* it?

The novel accurately conveys how isolated the victim of stalking comes to feel in society. As a result of one person's personality disorder, not one but two people become alienated from the wider social world. Like Joe

Rose, the victim of stalking begins to reflect profoundly on who they are and how they behave. Often they try to change. Some victims go so far as to change their name or alter their physical appearance. But more generally, all victims are forced to re-evaluate their way of dealing with social relationships. Why have they proved incapable of reasoning with someone? Are they sending out the wrong signals? Why did they make such a wrong choice of partner in the first place? It has to be said that uninformed cultural attitudes among the people who they turn to for support don't help here. When they hear about a victim's ordeal, some people may try and help them by joking that they should be flattered by all the attention, or should try making themselves less attractive. Rose's wife Clarissa becomes intolerant of his obsession with Jed Parry, suspecting him of being complicit in the crime because he has responded so obsessively to his persecutor's terrifying passion.

The increased self-consciousness of the stalking victim is neatly conveyed by an alternative to the term 'stalking' suggested by some psychologists: 'interpersonal terrorism'. Terrorists are so called not because of their specific political objectives nor methods, as both of these vary widely, but because their activity is designed to change the behaviour of a society, so that the everyday lives of its members are shadowed by fear. For terrorists to be successful, they do not need to carry out a particular threat: the threat may be enough. Following a terrorist act a society will undergo a lengthy period of self-examination, and the reassertion or alteration of its values. This is what has happened in the us and Britain in the years following the 9/11 and 7/7 terrorist attacks, where the soul-searching has revolved around questions of personal liberty and resulted in an assertion of less liberal values – as exemplified in the us 'Patriot Act' (2001) and the British government's drafting of the 'Terrorism Bill' (2005).

The result of *interpersonal* terrorism, similarly, is that we become self-conscious about areas of our lives we normally take for granted. How free ought we to be in society? Did we somehow bring what has happened to us on ourselves? How can we prevent it happening again? Stalking thus has a social and personal 'defamiliarizing' effect, causing us to reassess what we were accustomed to.

Stalking may be a crime that has existed long before it came to public attention in the 1990s, and it may be something that can affect the lives of anyone, no matter their age or gender. Nevertheless, the undeniable fact is that most victims of stalking are women; men only account for 10 per cent of victim statistics. This reminds us that although stalking is the definitive crime against the individual (it singles out one person and mercilessly persecutes him or her over a long period) it is also a social problem, and thus needs to be considered in the context of wider social issues, such as attitudes to women. For one thing this means acknowledging that prevailing cultural attitudes to love, as displayed in Hollywood films (I shall say more about this in chapter 4), play a role in motivating the stalker. As one psychologist drily puts it, when men are persistent in the movies they're just regular guys, and usually get the girl; when women are persistent, they are maniacs, and usually end up dead.[31]

But it also means recognizing that the way stalking is *experienced* by victims is also determined by their gender. As Orit Kamir says, stalking by a man tends to be felt as 'controlling, overpowering, oppressive and ever-present', while female stalking is 'repetitively returning, sexual, seducing, terrifying and guilt-inducing'.[32] The difference, she thinks, is because each kind of stalking serves a particular social function. Female stalking figures as a threat to the patriarchal social order, for it shows the dangers of 'undomesticated' female behaviour. Male stalking is way of reinforcing this social order, as it fulfils the patriarchal need to discipline both men and women, to keep everyone in their place through fear.

The rather alarming idea of stalking as an implicitly sanctioned mechanism for social control can explain the experience of stalking depicted in Margaret Atwood's remarkably prescient novels *The Edible Woman* (1969) and *Bodily Harm* (1981) (which even use the term 'stalking' in the sense we use it now). Each story is about a woman who is convinced she is being watched or persecuted in some way by a male friend or lover – but she can never prove this, and is regarded by others as paranoid and unstable. The implication is that stalking is not so much a crime perpetrated by a particular 'lone weirdo' but an inevitable social consequence of being a woman. Society may have changed a great deal since *The Edible Woman* appeared, but the familiar cultural double standards regarding female sexuality still operate. Women are encouraged to be 'sexy' and available, but must also be submissive, faithful, and unthreatening. When their sexual desires become too open or strong they represent a threat and must be controlled. When we consider the fact that your chances of being stalked are higher if you are a woman, there is the likelihood that this is because of our culture's prevailing misogyny as much as the disorders of individual men.

What's in a Name?

It is to some extent a cultural accident that we are left with 'stalking' as a name for the kind of behaviour I've been describing in this chapter, rather than any other. Certainly it's a term many psychologists are unhappy with, though they stick with it because it is too late to change now. Stalking is the word that happened to be used in relation to events that captured the public imagination at a particular time. It is possible to imagine that another term could have caught on in its place – a word such as 'persecute', for example, or 'sneak'. In Patrick Hamilton's 1932 novel about London low-life, *The Siege of Pleasure*, Jenny is looking for an excuse to get rid of the boy who is in love with her, when she realizes he has followed her to a pub: 'With grim delight she could see the case against him, and how she could thrust it home: "So you been sneakin' on me – have you?".[33] Other terms, such as prowling or lurking, or the old criminal charge 'loitering with intent' contain the combination of menace and stealth carried by the term stalking.

We must also remember that when it comes to analysing the terminology it is only English-speaking culture that uses the term 'stalking' so widely. Not all other languages have an overall 'umbrella' term for stalking behaviour, as we do. Some, such as German, borrow the English term (*der Stalking*), others try to confine the discussion to specific acts such as following someone or making threatening phone calls, or use more general terminology such as 'harassment' or the 'causing of fear'. The Norwegian anti-stalking law refers to 'frightening or annoying behaviour or other considerate conduct that violates another person's right to be left in peace'.[34] The medical historian G. E. Berrios points out that a French newspaper will describe stalking behaviour not by describing the actions with equivalents of the English term 'to stalk' like *traquer* (to track) or *suivre partout* (follow everywhere), but by emphasizing the state of mind of the perpetrator, calling him or her *'désaxé'*, the old French term for 'unhinged'.[35]

Nevertheless, it may be an accident, but there remains something quite appropriate about the English term 'stalking'. Alternatives like 'persecuting' or 'sneaking' do not imply the specific link between *two* people, subject *and* object, as powerfully as the word stalking. Nor do they suggest the idea of prolonged, systematic hunting, nor the sense of ghostly haunting, which is carried by the current definition of the term.

And the term is certainly here to stay, not least because it now has a clear *dynamic* potential. Using it can change the way we perceive of our relationships and our experience of society. This can be illustrated clearly by considering a curious dispute that blew up suddenly in the summer of 2003 in the pages of British broadsheet newspapers, involving the novelist Philip Hensher and the conceptual artist Tracey Emin. In an interview in the *Observer Magazine* Emin expressed her irritation by a comment Hensher had once made about her being too stupid to be a good conceptual artist, and told the interviewer: 'I responded. I'm not saying how, but I totally responded'.[36]

This mysterious admission led Hensher, in an article in the *Spectator*, to jump rather hastily to the conclusion that the person who had recently been harassing him by sending him unsolicited junk mail and porcelain figurines of Peter Rabbit addressed to one 'Phyllis Henshaw' might be Emin. Emin's response to being implicitly labelled a stalker was explicitly to accuse Hensher of stalking *her*. 'His obsession with me is pervy and creepy. I'm very unhappy and freaked out by all of this and I just want it to stop. He's coming from somewhere I don't understand; from weirdoland . . . he's been thinking about me, and imagining that I'm thinking about him. He's imagining me stalking him, and stalking me in turn through the media.' She threatened legal action.

Emin's protestation of innocence was vindicated when it turned out that another novelist, Paul Bailey, had been put through a similar ordeal to Hensher. This suggested that both men, as prominent gay novelists, were the victims of a homophobic stalker, and also – since Bailey had never written anything about Emin – eliminated Emin from suspicion. She later clarified that the mysterious response she had referred to was simply the fact that she had done a 'flattering' front-page interview with the very newspaper, the *Independent*, that had published Hensher's original critique of her art. But it is clear that the really effective retort was her accusation that Hensher was stalking her. Even though Hensher's accusation was closer to libel than stalking, the emotive implications associated with this term neatly emphasized the fact that she considered his criticisms unfairly personal, overstepping the boundary between acceptable criticism and unacceptable personal attack.

As well as unspoken social codes, stalking also violates real statutory laws. Having labelled Hensher a stalker Emin announced that her intention was not just to sue for defamation of character (the standard threat in critic-artist feuds) but to take out an injunction preventing him approaching her. Her comments underlined the fact that the term stalking carries with it real potential as a political weapon, as it opens up the possibility, not just of social stigmatization, but of legal action. Consequently, the row ended when the *Spectator* published a formal apology to Emin.

This rather odd story is really about the fickle sensibilities of artists and seems a million miles away from the real torment involved in stalking cases. But it does show how the idea of stalking operates as an 'interpretive frame' in our culture – a set of ready-made understandings about the way people relate to each other which we can apply to our own experience to make sense of it. The psychologists Mullen, Pathé and Purcell have argued in their book *Stalkers and their Victims* that the label 'stalking' is not just a replacement for previous terms like persecution or harassment, but nothing less than a new social construct by which we 're-frame' our experiences of being a social being. '[C]ertain types of interaction and certain forms of relatedness', they claim, 'have been changed forever'.[37]

In the clinic, the value of this is that victims of past persecution are now able to look back on their ordeal and derive a certain degree of comfort from regarding themselves as caught up in an established criminal phenomenon – one with recognizable patterns, outcomes and solutions. More generally, it means that everyone who thinks about stalking, either by reading a newspaper or watching a film, implicitly reassesses their opinions of themselves and their expectations of society. An analysis of the way that stalking highlights some of the faultlines of our society is what the next chapter aims to offer.

CHAPTER TWO

Stalking in Contemporary Culture

'I felt I was walking into a movie.'

John W. Hinckley, on his assassination attempt on Ronald Reagan, March 1981

What does stalking say about our culture? What kind of culture produces a crime like stalking and an individual like the stalker? Why do we watch and read films and books that depict disturbing acts of stalking? These are the questions I will try to answer in the rest of this book. Linguistic, legal and psychological definitions are valuable, but they can only take us so far. They point to the historical moment that stalking becomes a problem in society, what kinds of behaviour it involves, and to a certain extent what motivates it in a disordered mind. But they can't tell us *why*.

Since stalking was propelled into the public consciousness in the 1990s there have been an increasing number of academic studies of stalking. But very few of these deal with what we might call the *cultural* impact of stalking – the media response to stalking cases, and the huge numbers of films and books produced over the past decade and a half which have featured different kinds of stalkers or drawn directly on the premise of

45

stalking. These cultural representations of stalking are what I shall turn to most often in this chapter to try to answer the questions posed above.

The reason for this is that culture is a barometer of what preoccupies us at a given historical moment. This is especially true of 'popular' culture, or 'mass' culture – something that ought to be defined not in terms of its lack of quality or seriousness, but as the kind of thing large numbers of people actually consume everyday, the films we go to see, the novels we read. The philosopher Slavoj Žižek has suggested that we might regard pop culture today, so central is it to our everyday lives, as the equivalent of dreams in Freud's day, the 'royal road' which takes us directly into the unconscious. Just as the dream is a coded expression of desires and anxieties in the submerged individual mind, so the films we watch are evidence of what most secretly concerns us or excites us as a society.[1]

Stalking cannot be understood without recognizing its relationship to culture on a wider scale. As we have seen, stalking is fundamentally governed by the desire for intimacy and a corresponding inability to relate properly to another person. It is, in a sense, the definitive crime perpetrated by the individual against the individual. But rather than considering it in isolation, as if it is always a kind of private drama between two people, we need to consider how it relates to more pervasive questions of intimacy and the relationships with others in our culture.

Crucial here is the significance of the media. Although stalking really happens everyday, the fact is that it is also a media construct. In the previous chapter we saw that the media played a direct role in defining the modern concept of stalking, when the term first began to be used in the spheres of photo-journalism and newspaper reports of serial murder, and as a result of the moral panic about stalking in the late 1980s. Cultural production then ensured that the idea of stalking stayed in people's minds, through a succession of films, such as *Fatal Attraction* (1989), *Sleeping with the Enemy* (1991), *Pacific Heights* (1991), *Single White Female* (1992), *Stalking Laura* (1995), *Fear* (1996) and TV programmes like the series *Silk Stalkings* (1991–9), all of which directly depicted stalking behaviour.

But the influence of the media lies behind stalking in a more indirect yet even more powerful way. Media representation doesn't just straight-forwardly reflect what goes on in the wider world, as the films listed above might suggest (all were in some way 'inspired' by the moral panic about stalking and sought to depict a real-life phenomenon). Rather it actually intervenes in everyday reality and helps shape it. The appearance of stalking films in the early 1990s also *prolonged* the moral panic. But, more generally, reality itself is constantly filtered through media representation. This is not necessarily news to anyone in the modern world. It's obvious that the films or TV programmes we watch have a bearing on how we think of ourselves and how we relate to other people. The difference with stalk-ers, though, is that media representations, or more precisely the attitudes towards such things as love, intimacy, retribution, etc. which they perpet-uate, come to play a dangerously productive role in the fantasies which fuel their stalking behaviour.

Your Biggest Fan

The way that pop culture imprints itself upon those who live in it is most strikingly illustrated when we consider the role played by films, books, or songs in the stories of real celebrity stalkers, those who, by definition, have become fixated on their victim as a result of their response to media representations. Some become obsessed by one or two texts, around which a series of desires seem to have crystallized. With Mark Chapman, for example, it was *The Catcher in the Rye*. He became deluded that he *was* Holden Caulfield, the hero of Salinger's novel, who runs away from home as he comes to realize that the world is full of 'phonies'. Convinced that John Lennon was a phony, too, Chapman stalked and shot him. Other celebrity stalkers, like Robert Bardo, were shaped by a more indistinct *mélange* of references. Long before his fixation with Rebecca Schaeffer, Bardo had taken to writing letters, sometimes as many as three per day, to one of his teachers at school, each one signed with a cinematic *nom-de-plume*: 'Scarface', 'Dirty Harry Callahan', 'James Bond', etc. Clearly he was ready to play the role of vengeful lone hero when required. Perhaps this is why his own account of the murder of Schaeffer sounds so like a snatch of dialogue from a gangster movie: 'She had this kid voice . . . sounded like a little brat or something . . . said I was wasting her time! . . . I grabbed the door . . . guns still in the bag . . . I grab it by the trigger . . . I come around, and kapow, and she's like screaming . . . aaahhh . . . screaming . . . why, aaahhh . . . and it's like, oh God . . .' He also loved the U2 song 'Exit' (with its line 'the pistol weighed heavy . . .') and danced in court when it was played at his trial.

Other celebrity stalkers become obsessed by texts that are more directly linked to the people they stalk. Robert Dewey Hoskins's harassment of Madonna in 1995 revolved around meanings suggested by her own double-image – female religious purity as signified by her name, and the explicit sexuality of her clothing and songs such as 'Papa Don't Preach', which deliberately undercut this. Hoskins's original 'marriage proposal', a note he left for her after being turned away by her personal assistant, contained the words 'I love you. Will you be my wife for keeps. Robert Dewey Hoskins' but were scrawled on a printed religious tract entitled 'DEFILED' condemning those who fornicate outside marriage and those who go around without being properly clothed.[2]

No one would suggest that Chapman was directly inspired to kill Lennon because of a novel, nor that Bardo (who also carried around Salinger's novel) killed Schaeffer because Chapman killed Lennon, nor that Madonna was asking to be stalked because of the way she manipulated religious symbolism. All three men were diagnosed as having severe psychological disorders. But their actions were motivated by fantasies shaped by cultural narratives. It is not that watching a film or listening to music can suddenly turn someone into a stalker. It is more a question of damaged individuals, those who already have the capacity for violence and who feel alienated or disaffected, coming upon a cultural production which forms a crucial part of the fantasy structure which brings out their desire. The actual stalking behaviour, the symptoms of their psychic condition, can then be influenced by the particular details of the fantasy.

One film demonstrates this process at work more than any other. *Taxi Driver* (1976) is the story of the eponymous Travis Bickle, a lonely dislocated Vietnam war veteran who vents his rage against the decadent modern urban world he cruises around as he works. Paul Schrader's screenplay was partly inspired by the true story of Arthur Bremer's attempt to assassinate presidential candidate George Wallace on 15 May 1972, and the diary he kept (eventually published in 1974 as *An Assassin's Diary*) detailing his feelings of rage and inadequacy, and his plans for the murder. This formed the model for Travis's own journal, which is the basis for the voice-over in the film.

In turn *Taxi Driver* played a crucial role in motivating John Hinckley, the man who attempted to assassinate President Ronald Reagan in 1981 to impress Jodie Foster, whom he was stalking. His biography thus replays the dangerous double obsession represented in *Taxi Driver*: killing as a potentially redemptive act, and obsessive love for an inaccessible woman.[3] In his 20s, a socially impaired reclusive man, Hinckley became obsessed with *Taxi Driver*, watching the movie at least 15 times, listening continuously to Bernard Herrmann's scary soundtrack, and even dressing like Bickle in army fatigues and boots, and drinking the same peach brandy. He made up a girlfriend called Lynn Collins, based on the character of Betsy in the film, and wrote to his parents about imaginary trips he took with her. No wonder Hinckley felt, as he admitted at his trial, that he was 'walking into a movie' when he set off to assassinate the president.

Hinckley's trial was underpinned by a debate about the exact nature of the relationship between cultural texts and explosive personalities. The defence argued that Hinckley's obsession with *Taxi Driver* was largely unconscious, a way of salving his sense of isolation. They showed the film in court and Hinckley watched open-mouthed, only taking his eyes off it twice (tellingly, at the points when Betsy turns Bickle down and when Iris is embraced by his rival, Sport). Where the defence's point was that the film had exerted an unhealthy influence on a vulnerable viewer, the prosecution countered that the imitation of Bickle was deliberate and conscious, a way of firming up Hinckley's already psychopathic impulses, which would have led him to do what he did anyway. The defence won: Hinckley was found 'not guilty by reason of insanity' and incarcerated in a mental institution for life. Video rentals of *Taxi Driver* increased significantly after the trial.

You couldn't ask for a more potent symbol of the common view that films, books and songs are dangerous influences on dangerous people in our society, than *Taxi Driver* and U2's 'Exit' being played in court as evidence, as they were at the trials of Hinckley and Bardo. Such symbolism demonstrates that at such moments culture itself is in the dock, like some mysterious Mr Big pulling the strings behind the scenes of contemporary society. But Hinckley's story emphasizes that the relationship between the culture we consume and the way we behave is much more complex than that. What the continued immersion in a media-saturated world amounts to is nothing less than a weakening of the boundary between the exterior world and the interior self. We express ourselves through the films we watch and the music we listen to, the lines we quote and the episodes we remember. At times, it seems as if the world around us is in tune with our own thoughts and desires. This paranoid effect is an outcome of the way we are all caught up in a network of endless cultural references. It is not surprising that this should lead those who have real paranoid tendencies – like Hinckley and Bardo, and a great many stalkers – to respond in a dangerously extreme way.

Everystalker

In a very real sense, then, as these real-life cases show, culture produces stalking as much as represents it. Away from stalkers themselves, the general perception of stalking is also shaped by media representation – far more than formal legal or psychological definitions. If you were to ask anyone to describe the average stalker, the chances are that they would portray someone very like the figures of the stalker they have seen in the movies. It would probably be someone we could loosely characterize as a 'psycho' or a 'weirdo' – and would be either a single woman who wants a man but will turn nasty if she cannot have him, or a male loner who appears friendly at first but turns out to be weirdly obsessive. Both caricatures correspond to the most memorable stalkers as portrayed by Hollywood cinema in the last couple of decades.

First there was *Fatal Attraction*, which appeared in cinemas in 1987, a film which despite – perhaps because of – its depiction of a range of different pathological tendencies impossibly blended in a single individual, caught the public imagination as a terrifying representation of 'The Stalker' in our midst. More than any other film or book, *Fatal Attraction* rode the crest of a wave regarding stalking at the time. It tells of the systematic attempts of Alex Forrest – a stock 1980s type, the independent 'career woman' – to first possess and then destroy the man she had a brief affair with, Dan Gallagher, despite the fact that she started the liaison herself and promised him it would only be a one night stand. The film was widely regarded as accurately reflecting a growing sociological 'trend'. Numerous newspaper features appeared which analysed 'the *Fatal Attraction* phenomenon', telling real-life stories of men being harassed by vindictive women. The case of Amy Elizabeth Fisher, the so-called 'Long Island Lolita' who shot her lover's wife in the head in May 1992, was indissolubly linked with the film, so that her trial by a court was paralleled by a more brutal process of being, as one journalist said, 'charged with a movie' by the media.[4] In Britain, Robert Fine's stalker, whose relentless persecution of him in the late 1980s is detailed in his memoir *Being Stalked*, was described by the *Daily Star* as having 'a poisonous fatal attraction' for him, even though their relationship was quite unlike the one depicted in the film.[5]

Fatal Attraction affirmed Everystalker as a single woman, one with a voracious appetite not only for professional success but for sexual pleasure. What she wanted she got, and if this meant the break-up of a happy family, if this meant boiling pet rabbits, kidnap and even murder, then so be it. She was a danger to everyone: most obviously to men, who had to be careful whom they allowed to seduce them, but also to women, for she was out to get their partners and shatter their domestic bliss. The fact that this bogeywoman bore little relation, not just to clinical pictures of stalking behaviour, but to statistical evidence of stalking, was beside the point. In reality, a stalker was – and still is – much more likely to be either a vengeful ex-husband or ex-boyfriend out to punish their partner for being scared off by their brutal behaviour (as depicted in the film that is like a companion piece to *Fatal Attraction*, the 1991 Julia Roberts vehicle *Sleeping with the Enemy*), or a lonely under-achieving man (or woman) harbouring an obsession about a celebrity (as in the prescient Martin Scorsese films, *Taxi Driver* and *The King of Comedy* [1982]). Nevertheless, the caricature of the female stalker provided by *Fatal Attraction* is still relevant today, as shown when the term 'bunny boiler' crops up in the tabloids from time to time to refer to women who are apparently unhinged by desire.

An alternative candidate for Everystalker has recently emerged, however, encapsulated most faithfully in the film *One Hour Photo* (2002). This time he is male, close to middle-age, with no wife or family (or not any longer), a low-achiever, lonely and unloved. Although he is only marginally more plausible than Alex Forrest if we are looking for clinically accurate cinematic representations of stalkers, at least the film is a little more representative of the norm. In fact Parrish's very ordinariness is his key distinguishing feature. Played by Robin Williams at his most understated, Parrish is the quiet, nondescript photo developer in a large superstore, the kind of man you might share details of your life with as small talk while you use his service. This is just what one of his customers, Elena Yorkin, has been doing over the years when the film begins. But it turns out that behind the harmless exterior is a dangerous predator. Parrish has been surreptitiously collecting duplicates of the photographs he has developed for Elena, evidence of the secret desire he has to be accepted by her and her family, and which will erupt with murderous consequences by the end of the film.

Parrish's real nature is revealed in a scene which shows the stolen images arranged on his wall at home in chillingly obsessive detail. Versions of this scene have become something of a convention in depictions of the stalker or predatory killer on screen over the past couple of decades, up to the point of parody. It features in films such as *The Fan*, *The King of Comedy* and *Seven* and also in TV comedies such as *Bo' Selecta* and *I'm Alan Partridge*. The viewer is taken slowly, ominously, into rooms covered in photographs and souvenirs relating to the object of the stalker's obsession. This is visual code for the claustrophobic obsessed mind of the stalker, his most private realm, and an outward manifestation of the single-minded compulsion that drives him.

What *One Hour Photo* reveals is a fear which has characterized our perception of crime throughout the 1990s and into the early twenty-first century, the paranoid anxiety that a violent obsession lurks within the mundane exteriors of those 'others' with whom we share our world. Contemporary demons, the bogeymen of the mass media age, haunt our imaginations. The most monstrous of these is the serial killer, a figure Mark Seltzer has described as embodying the mass in a single individual (his amassing of victim after victim in similar 'trademark' style functioning as an ironic reflection of the culture of mass production). Serial killers are always remarked upon as being shockingly *ordinary*, just like you or I, able to blend into the crowd, with no one suspecting the depths of depravity that lie beneath their everyday exteriors. More immediate and tangible in everyday culture is the fear of the terrorist, who may be living quietly in a house nearby, planning for an attack, or the stranger loitering in the park, waiting to befriend our children – so often is the spectre of child abuse raised in the tabloids, on television drama, and on film.

One Hour Photo shows how our perception of stalking is underscored by a similar paranoia. What is disturbing about Sy Parrish is precisely the fact that he is not, until perhaps the very end of the film, the terrifying stalker-demon Alex Forrest becomes in *Fatal Attraction*. What unnerves us is the way his very normality conceals his abnormality. In fact what is abnormal about him develops out of a perfectly normal desire: to be loved. It is appropriate, too, that such an apparently normal family as the Yorkins should become his victims. The film expresses the fear not just that crimes are committed by apparently normal people, but that they happen to such quotidian families.

The fear of what apparent normality conceals also lies behind the power of *Fatal Attraction*, however, in a different way. The film is an expression of the anxieties which beset society in the late 1980s – the time of the AIDS panic, a ruthless corporate culture and a backlash against feminism – surrounding relations between the sexes. Its message was obviously that sex is dangerous, and stalking is presented as a kind of equivalent of a sexually transmitted disease, the lasting effects of an apparently frivolous encounter. But if we remove the film from the context of the 1980s and consider it in relation to later stalking films like *One Hour Photo*, what is striking is how it, too, depicts the hidden dangers of an apparently 'normal', everyday situation (albeit immoral and potentially damaging), where two adults who are attracted to each other decide to act on this attraction without hurting anyone else. It's the seductress who initiates the sexual liaison, promising 'no strings attached', yet it turns out that these rules count for nothing, or are replaced by a more mysterious set of rules which Dan cannot divine. So as much as the film is a warning to the promiscuous male about who he hits on, or even a cautionary tale about promiscuity itself in the climate of AIDS, it is also an expression of the fear that a mutually agreed contract might be meaningless. This, too, has a particular relevance to the ruthless corporate world of the 1980s, but it articulates a more general anxiety that social norms are in danger of collapse that is typical of more recent stalking films.

So here we have the two iconic figures of the stalker in our culture, the quiet male loner with a destructive violent core, and the ambitious independent woman, motivated by an excess of sexual desire. Neither bears much relation to authentic stalking-types (though, if we wanted to, we could see Alex Forrest as a 'former intimate' stalker and Sy Parrish a 'desired intimate'). Nor are they completely new characters (as if there ever could be such a thing in Hollywood cinema) but descend, in Sy Parrish's case, from the nobodies who want to be somebodies in Scorsese's films or from Patricia Highsmith's deceptively harmless heroes, and in Alex Forrest's, from a tradition of monstrous females, from the 'madwoman in the attic' in Victorian literature to the *femme fatale*. But both figures show how stalking has become one of a signature group of crimes – along with serial killing, terrorism, paedophilia – which serve as the focal point for a deep-rooted late twentieth and early twenty-first-century paranoia about the figure of the Other.

Yet compared to other crimes that make the everyday sinister, stalking has an extra twist because of its unique nature as a crime. Analysts have pointed out that what makes stalking extraordinary is, paradoxically, its relation to ordinariness, the fact that it

> may often consist of no more than the targeted repetition of an ostensibly ordinary or routine behavior. It does not apply to a distinct single action or actions: rather, it embraces a multitude of activities. Stalkers can harass victims using unequivocally illegal

actions, such as breaking and entering or committing acts of violence, but many stalkers do not overtly threaten, instead using behaviour that is ostensibly routine and harmless. Examples of this might include standing near somebody in a public place, or frequently walking past his or her house.[6]

This means, Robert Fine says, that the 'technique' of stalking (though it may seem an odd choice of word) is 'to turn the ordinary rituals of public life into instruments of oppression'.[7] Fine was the subject of a three-year stalking ordeal by an erotomanic former student whose behaviour mainly involved ostensibly harmless and law-abiding activities, such as waiting in her car outside his house or walking on the common nearby. As this took place in the years before the 1997 Protection from Harassment Act, there was nothing Fine could do about it – a fact his stalker showed herself to be arrogantly aware of. When he took the case to the civil court in 1996, the prosecution's strategy was therefore to insist on the cumulative effect of a series of events rather than (as her defence tried) to analyse individual incidents. This proved to be a landmark way of considering stalking, reflected in the 1997 bill. Individual actions may seem harmless in themselves, but it is the cumulative nature of stalking behaviour that distinguishes it as a crime.

Is there not something uniquely strange about a crime where that which is 'ostensibly routine and harmless' comes to seem threatening and full of hidden malice? Psychologists refer to 'hypervigilance' as one of the common symptoms among stalking victims, as they descend quickly into a state that resembles paranoia, aware that everyday existence has taken on a endlessly sinister aspect. Every time the phone rings, every time you check your e-mails, every time you return home, there is the potential for shock. Private spaces are transformed into possible locations for being terrorized; public spaces become pregnant with the potential for ambush. One of the bitter ironies of this 'paranoia effect' is the fact that stalkers are very often prone to paranoid thought disorder themselves. Their capacity to persist in their efforts to persuade a beloved person to succumb despite increasingly brusque rejections is often the result of their adherence to a delusional symptom.

But the fact that the victim of stalking comes in this way (if not in others) to be a mirror-image of their persecutor also points to an irony which operates on a larger scale. For as much as the stalker represents a menacing Other, a dangerous threat to normal life, he or she is also uncomfortably close to us. That is to say, stalking arises out of impulses and desires which are a *normal* part of relationships with other people: we all fall in love with people, we all admire people we know, even those we don't, like celebrities. It is also perfectly common for people to become disenamoured by those we were once close to, feeling wronged or frustrated. One of the striking things about Meloy's model of the 'narcissistic linking fantasy' is the fact that stalking is founded upon situations which are normal for anyone: the establishment of a 'narcissistic linking fantasy', followed by a rejection by the object of desire and subsequent feelings of shame or humiliation. Both of these are normal (if not things that happen everyday).

Significantly, and perhaps surprisingly, this paradoxical relationship, this underlying similarity between Everyman and Everywoman and Everystalker, is what recent Hollywood representations of the stalker trade upon by subtly causing us to empathize with the stalker figure. In films like *I Know What You Did Last Summer*, for example, we identify at some deep unconscious level with the stalker more than we feel for his victims. As I will argue in chapter Five, this is the result of the peculiar mechanism of cinematic identification between viewers and characters, and the conservative patriarchal nature of contemporary Hollywood.

One of the reasons we find stalking so eerily fascinating in our culture is that it is an intensification of our *normal* habits and emotions. No one would deny that stalking is driven by an extreme set of emotions and behaviours. It would also be foolish to try to minimize the traumatic consequences for the victim. But by delineating areas of extremity, implicit norms are tested and maintained. For, really, how do we *measure* what is 'normal' in any given situation? When does fascination with someone become unacceptable? When can the dogged pursuit of someone be legitimate?

The confusion about measurements and norms is articulated by Jess, the teenager accused of being a stalker in Hornby's *A Long Way Down*:

> I don't think you can call it stalking when it's just phone calls and letters and emails and knocking on the door. And I only turned up at his work twice. Three times, if you count his Christmas party, which I don't, because he said he was going to take me to that anyway. Stalking is when you follow them to the shops and on holiday and all that, isn't it? Well, I never went near any shops.[8]

The problem with determining what is normal in relation to stalking behaviour is one reason why the discourses surrounding stalking are so preoccupied with statistics. Robert Bardo possessed 100 videos of Rebecca Schaeffer. Tina Ledbetter was so disgusted that her idol Michael J. Fox got married that she sent him around 6,000 letters in two years – i.e. an average of 10 every working day. Helena Bonham Carter's stalker rang her up 16 times in a single minute. Thomas McCarthy estimated that he had followed 2,400 women. Statistics like these are proof of the excessive nature of the behaviour in question, the way it passes beyond the point of what might be considered 'normal'.

The Fragility of Social Laws

The fear of the abnormal lurking within the normal is complemented by another fear exposed by stalking. This is that the norms of behaviour to which we all adhere every day, and which ensure that social life is tolerable and not unduly threatening, are so fragile that they can easily be shattered when a stalker pushes against them.

The British director Christopher Nolan has said his film *Following* (2000), which tells of a writer who follows people to gain inspiration for his writing but before long becomes 'hooked' and eventually fatally persecuted himself by one of his quarries, was inspired by two things. First, there was the recognition of 'the voluntary protocols that a city like London has developed to preserve the individuality of people in close proximity to strangers. One example is that you don't walk at the same pace as a stranger if you're walking down Oxford Street or somewhere. It's very natural to vary your pace from a stranger, because otherwise it seems suspicious.' Second was his experience of being burgled. '[S]eeing a door broken down, you realize that the door wasn't ever keeping anybody out. When someone just decides to invade your space, it's really very shocking. I decided to put the two together. The one is the natural extreme, the logical extension of the other.'[9]

Nolan is referring here to the framework of social codes the sociologist Erving Goffman called 'civil inattention'. Sharing public space often requires behaviour that advertises clearly to those we share it with that we do not wish to interact with them, that we are not a threat to their privacy and that we respect them. This is why we stare into the middle distance rather than at other people in a public waiting room, for example, or, as Nolan says, walk at different speeds to strangers. But stalking is a kind of intrusive behaviour that violates this set of codes. As Robert Fine puts it, 'when the stalker looks into our windows, he reminds us of the fragility of the day-to-day conventions by which our experience of social reality and of ourselves is ordered and forces us to wonder why we do not see malevolence in any glance from another or any encounter on the street'.[10] Fine's ordeal at the hands of a stalker was exacerbated, he thinks, by the fact they first encountered one another in a university, an institution which is regulated more by implicit voluntary protocol than official sanction. His stalker was confused by the way university norms differ from those in the everyday world and 'misread' his openness and informality as sexual invitation.[11]

Stalkers wilfully or unwittingly misread such social codes. But victims of stalking like Fine are forced to re-assess the codes, and also consider whether they themselves have adhered to them correctly. Such is the effect of 'interpersonal terrorism', and it is exploited for dramatic effect by films like *Following* (2000) or a film released in the same year, *Un Ami Qui Vous Veut Du Bien* (translated as *Harry, He's Here to Help*). This story begins when a man, Harry, who claims to be an old schoolfriend of the hero, Michel, ingratiates himself into staying with Michel and his family at their holiday home for a few days. Though unfailingly smiling and courteous in the first half of the film, Harry's behaviour strains against the boundaries of what is considered socially appropriate from the outset: beginning with the slightly pushy way he gets himself invited to Michel's home, to his discussion of Michel's sex-life with a former girlfriend Claire is unaware of, and culminating in his purchase of an expensive new 4x4 for Michel to replace his broken down old car, despite Claire's protests that this gesture is 'out of proportion' ('*c'est disproportioné*'), and that 'People don't give and receive cars like that!'

The film was conceived by director Dominik Moll as a homage to Hitchcock, and before long Harry's behaviour becomes seriously threatening. Yet the way *Harry* invites us to consider what is proportionate socially or otherwise, how frail our unwritten social laws are, is its most powerful aspect. Social life depends upon everyone adhering to these tacit laws, but they are so easily broken. And once they are it is difficult to know how to act. Who can we appeal to, to preserve our safety? Later in the film, intuiting (correctly) that Michel's increasing moroseness and aggressiveness is the result of Harry's influence on him, Claire privately warns him to stay away from her husband. But her warning goes unheeded. That evening, Harry and his girlfriend Plum arrive with a box of champagne and presents for the children and the intrusions continue as before. At this point the viewer realizes that the story is not going to end until something horrible occurs, that, as Christopher Nolan says of his own hero, '[o]nce he's broken [one] rule, he breaks more and more'.[12]

There is a connection between the invisible tacit laws that regulate social existence and the much more visible statutory laws of human civilization, as passed by governments. But Moll's film underlines the fact that, in a way, breaking implicit social protocol is more problematic than outright crime. If someone commits what is obviously a crime against you or your property, at least you can go to the police. You can take them to court. But what if someone refuses to accept your demands that they remain within the social code?

The playwright David Hare once said that what he loved about the work of the novelist Patricia Highsmith is the fact that 'behind it lies the claim that, once you set your mind to it, any one human being can destroy any other'.[13] This is what happens in her well-known novel, *The Talented Mr Ripley* (1955), which details the systematic pursuit and elimination of one man by another. It is also a feature of less well-known Highsmith novels like *This Sweet Sickness* (1960) and *Those Who Walk Away* (1967), which also revolve around disturbing desires to possess and destroy. (It is why she has been called quite aptly, 'a balladeer of stalking'.[14]) Hare's comment about Highsmith neatly underlines the fact that even though her novels do not always feature stalking behaviour directly, they are all driven by one of its most disturbing features. One individual can easily terrorize another *if he or she sets his or her mind to it*. Or, more chillingly, we can turn the statement around: what ensures that most of us live in relative peace is the fact that someone else, one of the many other people whom we share our world with, both intimates and strangers, has *not* set his or her mind to terrorize us. The comfort of everyday social existence depends upon this simple equation. Although the odds are undoubtedly in favour of an unterrorized existence, it is still purely a matter of chance.

Celebrity Culture and Narcissism

What lies behind the whole question of civil inattention is the uncertain division between public and private space. A more literal way of asking questions about this issue than Christopher Nolan's or Dominik Moll's films can be found in the work of the conceptual artist Vito Acconci in the late 1960s and 1970s. His *Following Piece* (1969) drew on the stalking 'paradigm' at its most basic – one person following another. For the project he selected at random people on the streets in New York, and tracked them surreptitiously wherever they went, until they entered a 'private' space such as their car, office or home. Then he sent records of their movements and activities to various figures within the art world. The next year he performed his *Proximity Piece* (1970), which reduced the urban drama of *Following Piece* to the more confined space of the art gallery. This time he followed visitors around an art exhibition, eventually standing deliberately too close to his target. Then, sooner or later, they would move away.

Both pieces, in different ways, aimed to expose clearly one of the most significant and intangible boundaries which structures everyday life – namely the invisible lines which mark off our own private space within the wider sphere of public space. This is a mysterious aspect of social existence in the West (Eastern cultures have a different attitude to personal space), but it's essential to our cherished notions of freedom – and accounts for what would otherwise seem an absurd paradox in Nolan's comment about proximity in London, the fact that even in the throngs of somewhere like Oxford Street we feel we are still entitled to 'private space'. And what Acconci's experiments suggest is that that even though these boundaries exist and are valuable, when we compare them to the division between definite public and private *locations* (such as home, car, garden, etc. – which *Following Piece* respects), determining where they begin and end is much harder, they are much easier to breach and they are comparatively unprotected legally.

Measuring the private space we're entitled to in the public world is difficult, but there can be no doubt that it becomes more complex still when we take into account the way the world has changed even in the few decades since Acconci's performance pieces. In the age of the internet and advanced advertising techniques, the clearcut delineation of 'public' and 'private' space which governed *Following Piece* (city streets, shops, cafés, subway stations on the one hand, versus cars and homes on the other) seems almost quaint by comparison. People are now given the freedom to work from home, but the price of this is that mechanisms of workplace scrutiny enter their home. The media colonizes our everyday private space. Televisions are always on in the background, ensuring that lines from kids TV, soap operas, chat shows, advertising jingles etc., punctuate the moments of our daily lives. Twenty-four-hour news programmes filter our experience of the outside world, ensuring that we 'participate' in global crises, shaping our opinions about what is going on. We can be called up at home at any time of the day or night by telemarketing schemes, our private e-mail inboxes can fill up with unsolicited adverts, financial scams and pornography.

But one aspect of the contemporary world, in particular, has caused the notions of privacy and publicity to collapse into one another in a way that's relevant to stalking, and this is celebrity culture. The collapse is vividly illustrated in Martin Scorsese's extraordinary film about celebrity-worship, *The King of Comedy* (1982), the story of a wannabe stand-up comic, Rupert Pupkin, who is so determined to befriend his hero, chat-show host Jerry Langford, that he ends up kidnapping him and forcing him to let him do a routine on his show. For a nobody to become a somebody, the film implies, there can be no such thing as privacy. Because of his fame, Jerry Langford has had to forfeit virtually all of his private life. All his private spaces, car, office, home, are violated, one by one. And because of his craving for celebrity, the stalker Rupert Pupkin's private world is merely a fantasized public one. His most private space, his bedroom, is decked out like a TV studio, containing a huge blow-up photograph of a talk-show audience as it would look to a performer, and a mock-up of the studio complete with lifesize cardboard cut-outs of Langford and fellow guest Liza Minnelli. One of Pupkin's fantasies is being married live on air on the Jerry Langford Show, a neat prediction of the way that TV would, in the late twentieth century, colonize our private moments in the form of reality TV.

The film captures the point in recent history, two years after the shooting of John Lennon, when the dark underside of celebrity culture was beginning to become fully apparent. It is surely no accident that stalking enters the public consciousness as a result of the stalking of celebrities. Although statistically, more 'ordinary people' end up stalked than celebrities, and although stalking didn't begin with the harassment of celebrities but had been going on for centuries, stalking is nevertheless inextricably linked with celebrity culture.

Nowadays, stalking is not simply one of the hazards of achieving celebrity, but one of the devices by which celebrity is measured. The actress Jennie Kwan was once sent an e-mail which read 'Everyone knows you haven't made it in showbiz until you have your first obsessed fan.'[15] The British band Hear'Say, a product of the 'reality TV' music show *Popstars* in 2001 (reality game shows are almost entirely predicated on the lure of celebrity), were adjudged by the tabloids to have achieved fame when they realized they had their own stalkers. In another British reality programme, the 2004 talent show *The X-Factor*, one contestant, Cassie, spoke of having had a stalker even before she went on the show, but wondered why the man didn't pursue one of her 'gorgeous friends' instead. And when police began looking for a stalker who might be a suspect for murdering the British TV presenter Jill Dando, they received no less than 1,800 suggestions of potential candidates.[16]

Why do people stalk celebrities? The most obvious reason is that stalkers are attracted by the possibility of fame 'rubbing off' on them. In their trial – which often, naturally enough in a media-led world, is tele-vised by channels like Court TV – a stalker can momentarily cut an incongruous figure, dressed in a suit and neatly groomed, which contra-dicts the image of an unhinged obsessive which is central to the case against him. This is paralleled by a counter-reversal in which the celebrity victim, normally, by definition, someone who is at ease in the public eye, cuts a forlorn, distressed figure. During the trial of Robert Hoskins, Madonna protested that she felt 'incredibly disturbed' by the fact that the trial had 'somehow made his fantasies come true [in that] I am sitting in front of him and that is what he wants'.[17] Because of the nature of their crimes, celebrity stalkers can give the impression of enjoy-ing their day in court.

But the roots of celebrity stalking cases are more complex than simply the perpetrator wanting to be famous themselves, or enjoying their moment of infamy when it comes. For disaffected, lonely individuals, the promise of intimacy promised by a celebrity's image is powerfully attrac-tive and this causes them to reach out compulsively in return. In a world where they are constantly (like us all) bombarded by images of and messages from other people, potential stalkers can be struck by someone who appears out of the chaos and seems to be speaking directly to them, and whose image offers a way of somehow expressing the dissatisfactions of their lives. It is natural for those who feel inadequate to try and link themselves to a celebrity as a remedy.

This pattern stands out when considering the life of Barry Michael George, the man eventually convicted of the murder of Jill Dando on 26 April 1999. Much of the evidence against George was supported by a litany of obsessions he had had with different celebrities (as well as an enduring fascination with guns). At various times, he had called himself Paul Gadd, Gary Glitter's real name, pretended that the musician Jeff Lynne was his cousin, and changed his surname to Bulsara, in order to masquerade as Freddie Mercury's cousin.

Yet the fact is that celebrity culture encourages us all to feel like the cousins of the rich and famous. One of the most obvious effects of what Chris Rojek has called the 'celebrification' of our culture is that it encourages the fantasy that we can become intimate with those we have never met.[18] More specifically, celebrity culture works by trying to instill Meloy's 'narcissistic linking fantasy' in those who are designated watchers of the media show – i.e. all of us. Far from something pathological or even normal, we might argue that the narcissistic linking fantasy is an absolute ideal in our culture, its ideal state. Celebrities do not just go about their business trying to be successful when all of a sudden some maniac happens to entertain a fantasy about them. Being successful in contemporary culture, almost by definition, involves actively encouraging the fantasies of others. Becoming the object of obsession is the dark underside of what is in fact the standard process by which a celebrity reaches out to his or her audience (or market).

There are a number of strategies for seducing people into feeling they know a public figure intimately. One of the most common is for the star to present himself or herself as just like 'one of us', just a regular guy or girl. This helps explain the large incidence of stalking victims among TV presenters and chat-show hosts, those who, one would otherwise assume, occupy the less stellar region of the celebrity firmament. The English TV presenter, Sarah Lockett, herself a victim of stalking, has explained that the danger for the TV presenter is that, unlike actors who appear wearing the 'mask' of the character they play, the TV presenter addresses what he or she says directly to the viewer *as* him or herself; 'If you have an ad-lib or a funny story, that's genuinely your personality.'[19]

The US talk-show host David Letterman was continuously stalked by a woman called Margaret Ray in the late 1980s and early 1990s, who broke into his house, pottered around his toolshed and slept on his tennis court. His response was often to joke about the experience on his shows, allowing the viewers to share the problems in his life, as one might in a discussion amongst friends in a bar. But the irony is that it is precisely

Letterman's openness, his defining characteristic as a televisual personality, that made him especially vulnerable to stalkers in the first place.

Being an actor or a musician involves deliberately setting out to provoke an emotional response in viewers or listeners. Not surprisingly, film stars and singers constitute the two 'most stalked' kinds of celebrity. Stalkers might identify with the kind of characters that actors play, with the image of the 'real' person behind the roles, or feel that an artist's songs are directly for or about them. Mark Chapman regarded John Lennon's music (and that of others) as containing messages directed to him. He asked Lennon to sign his copy of his album *Double Fantasy* before shooting him – a grimly appropriate choice, for part of the delusional structure that drove him was the fantasy that he was Lennon's double. Despite being convicted for stalking country singer Barbara Mandrell over 15 years, the stalker John Carlson harboured an enduring ambition to perform in concert with her: 'I think we could do something like Johnny Cash and his wife. Barbara's songs tear my heart out. It's like she's calling me.'[20]

Of course the accessibility of the star is a carefully staged illusion. Once a member of the public – or the paparazzi – tries to get too close, the barriers between publicity and privacy are quickly lowered. This is one of the fundamental paradoxes of celebrity, summed up by the US radio comedian Fred Allen's well-known definition of the celebrity as 'a person who works hard all his life to become well known, then wears dark glasses to avoid being recognized'. Celebrity, as Chris Rojek has argued, further complicates an already problematic relationship between between the so-called 'I' (the real or 'veridical' self) and the 'Me' (the self seen by others via a form of staging or presentation).[21] Celebrities can feel a vast chasm between who they really are and the person they pretend to be, or may feel that the staged self dissolves the real one entirely.

This confusion between the desire to keep oneself away from the public and a simultaneous need to reach out to them is likely to fuel the stalker's ambivalent feelings towards the celebrity. The contradictions involved are depicted neatly in Tony Scott's film *The Fan* (1996). For the protagonist Gil Renard, being associated with a successful sports team is a way of securing some kind of achievement in a life otherwise marked by failure. His particular baseball hero, Bobby Rayburn, instinctively plays up to this by telling Renard on a radio phone-in how important the fans are to him. This remark is the cementing factor in Renard's narcissistic linking fantasy about Rayburn. Yet when eventually he is invited into Rayburn's beachfront penthouse he is appalled to discover that the star was lying. In fact he cares nothing for the fans '[b]ecause they don't understand that you're the same person, whether you're hitting it or you're not'. Rayburn dislikes the fans because they don't treat him as a real person. Naturally this revelation irritates Renard – and his irritation is intensified by the opulent surroundings of Rayburn's mansion, which emphasize how he has profited from the fans. Yet, ironically, this is the very moment when Rayburn *is* speaking as his 'real' self. It's just that his beliefs don't fit with the fantasy version of himself Renard has invested in. Rather than feeling privileged at the access he has gained to the real Rayburn, Renard is wounded to the core, as the revelation underlines his own lack of self-esteem. 'Without people like me', he tells Rayburn, 'you're fuckin' nothing'. He sets out to demonstrate this by kidnapping Rayburn's son and demanding that Rayburn save him by publicly dedicating his next home run 'to Gil, a true fan'. In the inevitable showdown that concludes the film Renard shouts to Rayburn as he pulls a gun on him: 'Now do you care?' The irony is one central to celebrity culture: the status of celebrity somebodies depends upon the fantasies of the nobodies who follow them.

It is important, however, to underline the fact that the narcissistic fantasy of connection with a celebrity is by no means the preserve of the deranged stalker. Celebrity magazines such as *Hello!* and *OK!* exist entirely in order to nourish the fantasy of getting to know celebrities as intimately as ordinary friends. The unprecedented outpouring of public grief following the death of Princess Diana in 1997, where people mourned on a mass scale as if a partner or relative had been killed, is a testament to the hold the 'narcissistic linking fantasy' can have on normal people and the way that the mass media demands that we indulge in it.

And, to an extent, we respond to celebrity with the characteristic doubleness of narcissistic fantasy, wavering between idolization and hostility. Our ambivalence can be engineered by the 'build you up, knock you down' treatment of stars by the tabloid newspapers. It is the source of the uneasy comedy of the British programme, *Bo' Selecta!*, which features its central character, the appropriately named Avid Merrion, literally stalking TV celebrities and forcing them to talk to him. Merrion is played by an actor (Leigh Francis), but this is never made explicit in the series. The result is that the boundary between playing the stalker and *being* the stalker is dissolved. At times, the stalked celebrities' confusion is apparent: they are reassured by the presence of the cameras that this is a genuine TV programme, but still feel themselves the victims of actual intrusion. This confusion is what explains our feeling of discomfort as we watch the show. Does *Bo' Selecta!* parody our stalking culture, or just contribute to it? Avid Merrion disgusts us, but eventually this disgust reflects back on ourselves at being implicated in this kind of culture. The programme's attitude to celebrity captures the ambivalence of our fascination with celebrities, the paradoxical mix of lust and hostility.

But there is nothing wrong with being a 'fan'. Fandom is a perfectly acceptable part of celebrity culture – and indeed something crucial to the economics of cultural production. Academics who study 'fan culture' distinguish between *followers*, people who are fond of something but not obsessed, and *fans*, those who are obsessed with a particular star, celebrity, sports team, film or TV series etc. and who assume some kind of social identity from their activity. But this kind of obsession is not considered dangerous. Some indeed regard it as a positive part of the mechanism of consumption that operates in popular culture. Fandom can be considered a 'performative act', a way of participating in the production of the film or TV series which is the object of its obsession, and keeping it 'alive' by continuing to generate new interpretations.[22]

The point at which acceptable 'fandom' tips over into unacceptable obsession was the starting-point for *The King of Comedy*, for it was inspired by the screenwriter Paul Zimmerman's amazement at a documentary about autograph hunters. He realized that 'autograph hounds are just like assassins except that one carries a pen instead of a gun'.[23] But the film underlines another fragile boundary which is crucial to the operation of celebrity culture, and to the stalking of celebrities: the distinction between fame and notoriety. Pupkin's plan to kidnap Langford and demand an appearance on his show succeeds, and Pupkin performs a 10-minute slot live, only to be apprehended and eventually sentenced to prison for six years. But part of the genius of the film is that we cannot quite be sure if Pupkin's routine is funny or not. And, in any case, the prime-time exposure Pupkin secures from the event guarantees that, upon release, he is famous. He publishes a biography and is eventually given his own talk show.

The film's ending thus casts everything that has gone on beforehand in sharp relief. Pupkin does turn out to be a success in the way that TV-driven celebrity culture might define the term: he is famous; he has his own show. This reminds us that quality is not at issue in celebrity culture; visibility and recognition are. Whether Pupkin is famous because of his talent or because of his criminal act of kidnapping is largely immaterial. And this makes the previous fantasy scenes in the film, where Pupkin and Langford chat over dinner as fellow celebrities (actually with Pupkin in the position of demanding superior) and where Pupkin, clearly an established comedian, is interviewed on the show, seem like plausible 'flashforwards' into the future rather than simply the delusions of Pupkin's younger self. His extreme efforts to become noticed may be recast – as we might imagine they would be in his bestselling memoir – as a simple reflection of what it takes to make it in showbiz in the late twentieth century, a measure of Pupkin's unwavering faith in his own genius.

In this way *The King of Comedy* asks what the difference is between a leftfield talent and a dangerously deluded individual. The answer, to all intents and purposes, is: *nothing*. It is purely down to how one is received by celebrity culture. What matters is not any inherent value, such as talent, but the place someone comes to occupy in the structure. Celebrity automatically confers upon someone at least a degree of social acceptability. We confront again here the indefatigable logic of stalking, that it is almost impossible to stop it working on its own terms. Stalkers who harass or attack celebrities do end up famous (albeit notorious), erotomaniacs like John Hinckley do end up 'an item' with the people they harass, who are never able to forget them.

The uncomfortable proximity between legitimate and illegitimate celebrity obsession is explored in the work of the Canadian artist Jillian McDonald, which takes as its focus her fascination with the Hollywood actor Billy Bob Thornton. The project stems, she says, from her experience of waking in the middle of an in-flight movie as Billy Bob Thornton and Cate Blanchett were kissing in the film *Bandits*: 'I knew immediately and irreversibly that I should be kissing him instead of her.' Visitors to her video installations and website, see clips of Thornton films into which McDonald has carefully inserted herself, replacing the actresses. Her web pages cleverly 'masquerade as a fan site' in order to help her explore the 'misplaced intimacy' which she regards as 'a symptom of our heavily mediated culture'. 'Via fantasy and extensive popular media', she says, 'the general public imagines secret affairs with favourite celebrities. The crush is a familiar experience.'[24]

In a very real sense, then, celebrity culture *is* a stalking culture, one that is geared up to producing the kind of 'misplaced intimacy' explored in McDonald's work. It legitimizes kinds of stalking behaviour. Fandom, as exhibited at conventions or via fansites on the internet, is one example.

Another is the paparazzi, an entire apparatus constructed around the desire for intimacy with celebrities. As celebrities have tried to control their image more and more, by employing an expanding arsenal of managers, minders and PAS, so photography of the celebrity has shifted to the arena of the 'stolen' snapshot, thus relying ever more on the profession that resorts to stalking behaviour (as well as a new breed of amateur paparazzo – members of the public armed with digital cameras). The blurred distinction between the 'legitimate' need to get close to stars and 'illegitimate' stalking behaviour is highlighted in the ironic conclusion to Jay McInerney's novel *Model Behavior* (1998) when the protagonist, Connor McKnight, a newspaper 'celebrity correspondent', is shot by his stalker – a young woman determined to become a model. Rumours have been planted that accuse McKnight of being a 'kind of loner, a bit of a weirdo' and stalking a filmstar, when in fact he has been trying legitimately to get access to him for a magazine feature.

But the dangerous intertwining of stalking and celebrity culture cannot simply be envisaged as a one-way relationship, a straightforward matter of deluded stalkers preying on those more rich and beautiful than themselves. Celebrity is complicit in the creation of a narcissistic linking fantasy, and because fantasy is such a powerful force motivating our behaviour, there is always the potential for this to lead to trouble. Moreover, as the ending of The King of Comedy so powerfully shows, it is not as if becoming famous is a rational, regulated process which assesses an aspirant celebrity's qualities according to set norms. Celebrity involves reaching out to an audience, it involves exposure and exhibitionism. To stay in the public eye, a celebrity needs to keep what passes for his or her 'real self' on display. Is it so surprising that some damaged individuals mistake this self-exposure for an invitation to penetrate further into that self?

This curious logic of equivalence – because you expose yourself I have the right to become intimate with you – may be what explains the bizarre story I considered in the previous chapter, where two artists accused each other of stalking without any evidence whatsoever. Wasn't what lay behind Philip Hensher's accusation about Tracey Emin the mistaken equation between the impulse towards obscene self-exposure and the urge to enter forcibly the life of another? Emin's art, more perhaps than any other artist, is one that trades on the exhibitionist logic of celebrity culture, governed by the impulses towards false intimacy and self-exposure. Perhaps it's not so inconceivable that an aesthetic which can produce a piece entitled Everyone I've Ever Slept With could also encompass stalking. After all, many artists – not just Vito Acconci, but also Sophie Calle in her Venetian Suite, and others such as Sherrie Levine – have produced work based on real acts of stalking or which evokes obsessive pursuit.[25]

Stalking and Postmodernity

As a fundamentally narcissistic disorder it is also quite appropriate that stalking emerged just as the time when cultural critics like Christopher Lasch were describing contemporary society as deeply narcissistic. Lasch argued in his book *The Culture of Narcissism* (1979) that the combined effects of capitalism (which values the manipulation of other people over intimate, caring relationships), commodity culture (where the consumption of objects is the answer to every problem), and the dominance of the electronic image (which means what we see around us are not so much *other* people or images, but things whose appearance is distorted by what *we* project onto them), replicates in the inhabitants of the modern world the condition of pathological narcissism. Modern existence is like living in a world of mirrors, constantly being aware of scrutiny and invited to scrutinize others in return. Psychoanalytically speaking the mirror effect serves to dissolve the boundaries between subject and object, and internal self and external world. There is thus a parallel movement in both individual and society: where culture is dominated by the logic of the mirror, the obsession with surfaces, the ethos of competition and control over others, so narcissistic personality traits characterize many of the people who live in this world.[26]

This parallel movement emphasizes the fact that while it is right on one level to regard stalking as an 'old behaviour' which demonstrates how fragile *universal* social codes and cultural norms are, the phenomenon is also absolutely in tune with the nature of our culture *now*, at this point in our history. Surely it is more than a coincidence that a crime predicated on the inability or unwillingness to observe the rules of social interaction should become prevalent at precisely the time when these rules are becoming less stable?

Our 'postmodern' world is characterized by a widespread lack of consensus about cultural norms and prescribed standards of behaviour. We no longer look to nature, tradition, social customs or official laws in order to determine how we act. The widespread decline in religion is one of the principal reasons for this, as with it goes a simply-adhered-to moral framework against which to consider or to judge our actions. But it has been paralleled by a loss of faith in other structures that provide authority, such as politics and family life. We don't vote in large numbers any more, we are sceptical about politicians and their pronouncements, and the traditional family cannot be espoused unproblematically as an ideal.

An overall climate of 'permissiveness' characterizes contemporary existence. This word has inevitable reactionary connotations, and I don't want to pretend that the decline of religion or the nuclear family is necessarily something to mourn. One only has to replace the word 'authority' with 'patriarchy' and we can appreciate the benefits its decline might bring for some members of society. Yet we have to acknowledge that the shift in the attitude to authority that typifies postmodern culture is at the very least a mixed blessing. For while it has empowered or liberated some, it has undoubtedly led to uncertainty about how we should act in particular circumstances, which rules we should follow in certain situations, perhaps even whether there are rules in the first place. This uncertainty is undoubtedly a factor in stalking. It is not that stalking is produced *directly* from the uncertainty about how to initiate, participate or even respond to rejection in a particular relationship. For someone to become a stalker there has to be, as we have seen, a pre-existing pathological psychic structure which is then 'triggered off' by the particular way a relationship develops. But in certain individuals, an uncertainty about how to behave in relationships, an inability to take full account of how their actions transgress what is normal, is a crucial contributing factor in their turn to stalking.

To acknowledge this means rethinking the connection between stalking and authority. One of the common arguments about stalking is that it is effectively a patriarchal social mechanism. Orit Kamir contends that the differences between 'male' and 'female' stalking come down to different ways of responding to the patriarchal order. Female stalking is a threat to the patriarchal social order because it shows the dangers of 'undomesticated' female behaviour. Male stalking, on the other hand, operates as a version of the desire to police and punish women that shapes many aspects of our culture. Stalking thus 'effectively frightens men and women into social roles designed for them, subordinating them to the ruling ideology, ruling classes and ruling deity'.[27] We can see this at work in contemporary cinema, if we compare *Taxi Driver* and *Fatal Attraction*, each of which features an archetypal version of, respectively, the male and female stalker. Where *Taxi Driver* portrays the disaffected, symbolically emasculated, male stalker trying to wipe the scum off the streets and ultimately being congratulated for it, the latter demonizes the female stalker as an example of the dangers of unfettered sexuality in the accumulative, aspirational late 1980s.

Kamir's theory is valid up to a point: the majority of stalking victims are woman, and most stalkers men. Their crimes can be seen as reinforcing prevailing gender stereotypes. But it simply isn't tenable to describe our social world straightforwardly as a 'patriarchal order' any more. Without doubt, misogynist attitudes still prevail. But if the general attitude to authority has changed, it follows that patriarchy cannot function in the same way as before. Slavoj Žižek has insisted that the decline of traditional forms of authority doesn't mean that authority has simply vanished, and anarchy reigns. Instead what has happened is that a more complex, devious and covert kind of authority prevails, one that urges us to go beyond what Freud called 'the pleasure principle'.

Freud's term is often mistaken for a hedonist call to arms, an advocation of the values of a decadent lifestyle. But really it is about the fact that for society to function smoothly, i.e. without anarchy, its members must *regulate* their pleasure, taking *just enough* pleasure to satisfy themselves – and pleasure of a kind which is socially acceptable. Too much pleasure can become a threat to social order. In our permissive 'postmodern' liberal democracy, however, the rigid authoritarian laws which prohibit unacceptable behaviour and preserve the pleasure principle are supplanted by a covert set of rules which urge us to go beyond the pleasure principle, urge us to indulge our impulses towards pleasure-seeking, especially sexual ones, to take enjoyment from whatever we do. Conversely, our apparent freedom, according to Žižek, masks a whole set of 'hidden prohibitions'. On the face of it we seem to be able to say or do what we like, but soon find out that there are implicit limits.

It is this paradoxical model of authority which provides an important context in which to consider the modern stalker, the Everystalker of our times. It doesn't directly 'create' him but helps shape him. He is the recipient of mixed messages. On the one hand, he looks for guidance about how he ought to act in certain situations, but finds none is forthcoming. He may take it upon himself to act as a kind of agent of patriarchal law, a kind of second-in-command, over-zealously hammering home the lessons he feels his master has failed to apply – the model of male stalking, in other words, described by Orit Kamir. On the other hand, immersed in a world where advertising, films and newspapers constantly emphasize that anyone can – and indeed ought to – have it all, he feels left out, and seeks to do something about it. His stalking might be considered the result of obeying the implicit message to pass beyond the pleasure principle: 'in a world in which one is entitled to anything, why can't I have *you*?'

CHAPTER THREE

Enter the Stalker

[T]he concept of 'strolling', aimless urban wandering, the *flâneur*, had been superseded. We had moved into the age of the stalker; journeys made with intent – sharp-eyed and unsponsored . . . The stalker is a stroller who sweats, a stroller who knows where he is going, but not why or how.

Iain Sinclair, *Lights Out for the Territory* (1997)

J. Reid Meloy has called stalking 'an old behaviour, but a new crime'.[1] This claim is easy to verify by casting a fresh glance at stories of love gone wrong from previous historical periods. The nineteenth century, in particular, sees a wealth of tales that resemble modern stalking cases – only of course they don't involve a court.

Lady Caroline Lamb's behaviour once the legendary womanizing poet Lord Byron had tired of their passionate affair, for example, bears all the hallmarks of 'former intimate' harassment. Beginning with constant letter-writing and unaccompanied visits to his home (a scandalous thing for a woman to do at this time) her actions became more and more desperate and persecutory. On one occasion she sent him a clipping of her pubic hair, on another she wrote in a novel lying open on his desk 'Remember me!' (Byron responded by writing a short poem with this title, which assures her ironically he won't forget her.) In July 1813 Lamb brandished a knife in front of him in public, cutting her hand. Then she spread unfounded stories about his having an incestuous relationship with his half-sister and sexual relationships with boys. Byron never spoke to her again – and this almost caused her to go mad, for her obsession never ended. In 1820 she appeared at a masked ball as 'Don Juan', shortly after publication of Byron's poem of that name.

In 1818 the French writer Stendhal (real name Henri Beyle) fell hopelessly in love with an Italian woman, Mathilde Dembowski. For three years he besieged her with letters and personal visits to her home in Lombardy hoping to persuade her to return his love, but she always resisted. His rather inept attempts at seduction included disguising himself in an overcoat and dark-green glasses and following her about. Given the sensitive political context (at this time Lombardy was ruled by Austria as a virtual police state) Stendhal's furtive methods led to suspicions that he was a French government agent. Eventually he achieved catharsis through writing his book *De l'Amour* in 1822, an analysis of love that nowhere mentioned Dembowski but was motivated by his unrequited passion for her.

Then there is the case of Adèle Hugo, daughter of the French writer Victor Hugo, who had an erotomanic obsession with a British naval lieutenant. She ran away from home in 1863 to pursue him to Nova Scotia, Canada. When he tried to escape, she followed him to the Caribbean too. The story was uncovered when her coded diaries were found in 1960 and documented in the 1975 François Truffaut film, *The Story of Adèle H.* In the film, at first she pursues Lieutenant Pinson around the town, persuading him that her love would be good for him. Then she spies on him when he is with his mistresses, before beginning more seriously to try to embarrass him: she orders a prostitute for him, offers publicly to settle his gambling debts, and arranges for a marriage notice to appear in the press, in the hope of forcing him to marry her for fear of scandal. Eventually she wrecks Pinson's engagement by revealing his previous relationship with her to his fiancée's parents, and lets it be known – mendaciously – that she is pregnant with his child.

Stalking has been called 'the crime of the 1990s', but these examples suggest that it is a behaviour equally typical of the nineteenth century – especially when we take into account instances from nineteenth-century fiction. There's William Guppy's lengthy amorous pursuit of Esther Summerson in Dickens's *Bleak House* (1853), for example, or Louisa May Alcott's 'lost' first novel, *A Long Fatal Love Chase* (1866), where the heroine is pursued relentlessly by a Rochester-like husband who refuses to accept that their marriage is over and becomes more and more angry and vindictive the longer she tries to escape him. But for all the prescience of nineteenth-century culture are we really justified in calling the behaviour it depicts *stalking*? And is there any value in doing so?

I think there is, even though we can become prone to the peculiar kind of narcissistic blindness that can affect the historian, unable to recognize that what we take to be an accurate picture of the past is actually our own reflection mirrored in what we see. Psychological analyses of stalking at times fall into this trap. One writer assesses Shakespeare's sonnets by asking, rhetorically and simplistically, 'Was Shakespeare a stalker?'[2] Others contend that the obsessive pursuit in Dante's *Vita Nuova* is remarkably similar to a modern stalking case.[3] Gregory Dart has gone as far as complaining that this kind of wilful obliteration of the distance between past and present is, ironically, similar to 'the sense of entitlement, the assumption of false intimacy, that is at the heart of stalking'.[4]

Yet looking back at literature of a previous historical era can help us understand the horizons of conception at a particular moment. It can tell us what could be conceived of, and, more importantly, *how* it was conceived. Looking back at depictions of stalking behaviour before they were recognized as such – looking at stalking before 'stalking', in other words – can help us to understand the roots of stalking as a modern social phenomenon. But to avoid historical blindness, it is important to take properly into account the context of the stalking behaviour. To read a hidden stalking subtext into Shakespeare's sonnets overlooks the crucial element of masquerade in sonnet-writing (especially in Shakespeare's case). To become suspicious about Dante's intense passion fails to consider the medieval convention of 'courtly love'. We ought to confine ourselves to those episodes and stories which are presented in such a way that they point to an underlying attitude which is similar to the way we conceive of stalking now. It is not enough for a story to involve obsessive pursuit; the relationship between two individuals needs to have the whiff of something pathological or criminal about it. William Guppy in *Bleak House*, for example, is obviously a nuisance to Esther Summerson, but he is not portrayed as dangerous or mad.

It is a different matter in a later Dickens novel, however. One of the stories in his sprawling work *Our Mutual Friend* (1865) is about Bradley Headstone, a self-made school teacher, who falls in love with Lizzie Hexam, an illiterate young girl who he has tried to teach to read. Scared off by his intensity, she rejects his awkward proposal of marriage. As sometimes occurs in modern stalking cases, Headstone's subsequent rage is not aimed directly at punishing Lizzie, but the man he sees (rightly, as it happens) as the rival for her affections, the gentleman Eugene Wrayburn, whom he despises and who is openly scornful of Headstone's position lower down the social ladder.

In a chapter called 'Scouts Out' there begins a grotesque nightly choreography where each evening Wrayburn goes out on a stroll after dark (just like Dickens himself, in fact, in his famous 'nightwalks') and is followed by Headstone. Sometimes he walks, sometimes he takes a cab, but he is sure Headstone is always tailing him. At certain points he deliberately turns back on himself before Headstone has time to hide, so that he can pass him as if 'unaware of his existence'. He goes to bed each night knowing that Headstone is outside watching. Wrayburn is so self-assured that he professes to enjoy the whole procedure, describing it to his friend Mortimer Lightwood as hunting, 'the pleasures of the chase', and speaking of the locations for the nightly ritual

– 'there is rather difficult country around Bethnal Green' – as if venues for a rural chase.[5] The episode, significantly, fuses the original and later uses of the term stalking, as human being becomes animal prey.

Wrayburn's jokiness emphasizes the black comedy of the whole business, but the implications of the hunting metaphor also suggest – as Lightwood recognizes, being much more alarmed at the nightly pursuit – that it will end with a death. Sure enough, many months later, after tracking Wrayburn relentlessly over London, Headstone sneaks up behind him after overhearing him try to persuade Lizzie to marry him and bludgeons him over the head with a broken oar, leaving him for dead.

In its menace and violence this story feels so modern that it seems incongruous as a nineteenth-century text. But Dickens can have this effect: he is often fêted for his prescient depictions of an unmistakably modern criminal mind. In this case, there are two significant features about the obsessive pursuit in *Our Mutual Friend* that suggest we can see the novel as one of the earliest modern depictions of stalking. The first is the fact that what happens to Eugene Wrayburn is explicitly linked to Headstone's inherently criminal nature. The narrator says of him:

If great criminals told the truth – which, being great criminals, they do not – they would very rarely tell of their struggles against the crime. Their struggles are towards it. They buffet with opposing waves, to gain the bloody shore, not to recede from it. This man perfectly comprehended that he hated his rival with his strongest and worst forces, and that if he tracked him to Lizzie Hexam, his so doing would never serve himself with her, or serve her . . . And he knew as well what act of his would follow if he did, as he knew that his mother had borne him.[6]

The implication is that, in someone like Headstone, a man who seems naturally to be a 'great criminal', feelings of love and rivalry will inevitably lead to criminal acts. Indeed falling in love has been experienced by him with nothing short of anguish. For someone who has had to work so hard to keep his natural emotions suppressed to ensure social advance, falling in love is a threat to his self-control. This is why Headstone's declaration of his love for Lizzie, though passionate, takes the form of an aggressive verbal attack. He tells her straightforwardly that he loves her, but this simple confession is buried amongst statements such as 'You are the ruin of me', 'I have never been quit of you since I saw you', 'you could draw me to the gallows' etc.[7] It is not an object lesson in the seductive arts.

The second key feature of this novel is the way that it presents the city, especially at night, as the locus for stalking behaviour. Surrendering himself to the sights and sounds of the gaslit metropolis was a pleasure Dickens indulged in in his nightwalks. This is a pleasure Wrayburn shares, but Headstone's brooding presence means that in *Our Mutual Friend* the freedom of walking in the city becomes tinged with menace. The implication is that the city streets provide the framework for an obsessive pursuit that leads inevitably to violence, like the tracks on a tramway. The city is what intensifies the proximity between individual and the threatening *other*.

Stalking in the Nineteenth-century City

Dickens's interest in the 'great criminal' and the inevitability of his crime is typical of an attitude towards crime which develops throughout the nineteenth century, and is a significant factor in the eventual 'official' emergence of stalking nearly one hundred years later. Michel Foucault argued that the powerful emergence of the psychiatric discourse throughout the nineteenth century meant that crime became increasingly pathologized. It was no longer regarded as proof of moral weakness but evidence of mental disorder. The result was that, by the end of the century, penal law no longer revolved around the criminal *act* but was geared towards assessing the level of criminality of an *individual* in order to determine his or her likely danger to society. Consequently, late nineteenth-century culture is haunted by the spectre of what Foucault calls the 'Dangerous Individual', a kind of fantasy-figure who threatens social stability: 'from the rare and the monstrous figure of the mono-maniac to the common everyday figure of the degenerate, of the pervert'.[8]

It is clear that something similar occurs with the invention of the category of 'stalker' in the late 1980s and early 1990s. The stalker is one of late twentieth-century culture's 'dangerous individuals', along with the serial killer, the paedophile and the terrorist. But the example of *Our Mutual Friend* suggests that the nineteenth century is when stalking as we conceive it now begins to seep into the cultural unconscious. At various points throughout this century, a small space was being carved out in the cultural imagination for another dangerous individual, the stalker.

Surely it's no accident that the nineteenth century sees, within the gothic tradition of literature, the flourishing of powerful new imaginings of what Orit Kamir considers the 'archetypal' male stalker figures. Kamir's view is that the figure of the stalker can be traced back to prevailing cultural archetypes, such as Lilith, a dark and transparent vampirish demon who roams around stealing babies and seducing men against their will and knowledge, and God, Satan and Faust, her male counterparts, watchful, ever present, unseen, controlling.[9] Two especially pertinent versions of this figure emerge towards the end of the century. The first is Robert Louis Stevenson's Mr Hyde (1888), who stalks women and also (like Frankenstein's monster) his own progenitor, Jekyll himself, entirely unable to control his impulses. Then there is Bram Stoker's Dracula (1897), the prototypical serial-killer stalker, linked in the public mind with the Ripper murders nine years before as a kind of 'eternal Ripper'.[10] Significantly, despite his supernatural qualities, he too is described as 'a criminal and of criminal type'.[11]

What differentiates these figures from other 'archetypal' stalker-figures (like Faust or Frankenstein's monster), what makes them more like ancestors of the modern stalker, is that the nature of their pursuit seems entirely at home in the city. The nocturnal metropolis is their natural habitat – they prowl around the dark alleyways, lurk in the shadowy streets, immune to the sense of menace felt by others. This element of urban realism, of existing amongst real human beings in places we all recognize, is important. For although there's something monstrous about our own fictional versions of the stalker (think of Alex Forrest in *Fatal Attraction*) there's also something human and unhinged about them: they are not supernatural figures motivated purely by evil, but damaged people compelled by an excess of warped desire. It is their very humanity that unnerves us, not their monstrosity, the fact that they're unable to control themselves.

The combination of being at ease in the city and being under the grip of obsession is what's so striking about Dickens's Bradley Headstone. But it's even more significant in an earlier, and much more slender, nineteenth-century text, Edgar Allan Poe's short story 'Man of the Crowd'. This story, published in 1840, deserves, more than any other, to be seen as the archetypal modern stalking story. It may be less revealing about the psychology of the stalker than Dickens's novel, but it links together more forcefully obsessive pursuit, crime, and the modern metropolis. 'Man of the Crowd' implies that stalking behaviour is an inevitable consequence of *modernity*, for its tale of stalking is played out against an urban backdrop that symbolizes the lawless spaces of modernity. It depicts at its purest the fundamental *structure* of stalking, its basic 'choreography', if you like: two human beings engaged in an intense pursuit that resembles a kind of duel or deadly game.

'Man of the Crowd' was described by Walter Benjamin as an 'x-ray picture of a detective story'.[12] But it is also an x-ray version of every stalking story. The tale has no real plot, but is an extended motion picture in words. It begins with its convalescent narrator sitting by a coffee house window in London looking out at the crowds on the streets outside. Soon, though, he spots one particular figure, an old man, who fascinates him. Stricken by a 'craving desire to keep the man in view – to know more of him', the narrator then pursues him doggedly until the next evening, becoming more and more agitated. The pursuit lasts for as many as 24 hours. Eventually he gives up, deciding – as the famous conclusion to the story has it – that '[t]his old man . . . is the type and the genius of deep crime. He refuses to be alone. He is the man of the crowd'. He thus represents the impenetrable heart of darkness of the modern world, a world which, as the German quotation used by the narrator has it, '*er lässt sich nicht lesen*' (it does not permit itself to be read).[13]

The story is founded on a paradox which results from the advent of the great city in the nineteenth century. City life sees the individual being placed next to his or her 'other' in a particularly vivid and direct sense. Existing alongside a diverse community of strangers, with different backgrounds, value systems, nationalities, etc., forces the inhabitant to acknowledge how *different* individual people are from each other, how mysterious to one another, too. But at the same time the growth of the city introduces another way of thinking the human besides the difference between individuals. The explosion of urban population heralds a new sociological category: the mass. The crowd of people seems to have its own amorphous individuality, seething with purpose like a single human being. And the paradoxical singularity of the crowd means that the threatening other might *not* be visible. A 'dangerous individual' might be lurking there, able to take advantage of its cloak of anonymity.

The urban crowd thus has a paradoxical doubleness: individuality is both accentuated and dissolved. The city manages to dispel fear and suggest unity by giving the impression of a mass of humanity engaged in a similar purpose. But it also exacerbates the anxiety that the threatening other might be engaged, undetected, in criminal behaviour. The crowd is the tangible manifestation of this paradox, as it is something we can all see, hear and feel. Not surprisingly, Poe was just one of many nineteenth-century writers who sought to convey the social significance of the modern city through the metaphor of the crowd.[14] Another is the French poet and commentator on modernity Charles Baudelaire whose work encapsulates the idea of the city's doubleness even more directly. Baudelaire depicted the crowd as at once bestial and beautiful. He revelled in the idea of the crowd as a kind of outward symbol of modernity itself, which he famously defined as 'the ephemeral, the fugitive, the contingent, the half of art whose other half is the eternal and the immutable'.[15]

What Baudelaire often does is focus on one particular individual who momentarily stands out from the mass, a kind of fantasy figure who teases out his desire for intimate connection. His poem 'A une passante' (1857) ['To a passer-by'], for example, tells of a brief encounter on the street with a tall, slender woman in mourning dress. She is treated by the narrator as someone with whom he shares a special, mysterious connection. He says: 'Of me you know nothing, I nothing of you – you / whom I might have loved and who knew that too!' Gregory Dart has suggested that this strategy is by no means unique to Baudelaire, but something that city-dwellers naturally employ. He calls it a 'fantasy of particularity', the point of which is to create a kind of 'antidote' to the dehumanizing effects of the urban mass. Faced with something vast and abstract, quite unlike an established community with a network of personal relationships, the inhabitant of the city takes refuge in imagined idealized encounters with the other in the modern crowd, and thus feels reassured that individual uniqueness can survive. This seems like a natural defence mechanism of the social being, but, in Dart's view, this 'fantasy of particularity' is also one of the roots of modern stalking behaviour. Stalking, he thinks, 'is nothing but an extreme version of this fantasy'.[16] The crowd continuously provides the city dweller with tantalizing experiences of artificial intimacy and proximity which prefigure the more widespread conditions of modern media culture as they were to develop in the late twentieth century.

This insight into the link between stalking and the modern urban world is made stronger by what Dart does not consider. An alternative to the fantasy of intimate connection triggered by the experience of the crowded city is the fantasy of imagined enmity. The anonymous other is not just the object of artificial affection, but of the paranoid fear that the other might destroy everything one stands for. Just as a special, desirable individual might be concealed by the crowd, so a menacing figure might be hiding there too. It is this paranoid counterpart of the fantasy of particularity that underpins Poe's 'Man of the Crowd'. A blackly comic variation would be the stalking episode at the heart of Dostoevsky's study of urban alienation, *Notes from Underground* (1864). The Underground Man doggedly tracks down an army officer who he feels has insulted him in the past by acting indifferently towards him, and takes to walking down the sunny side of the Nevsky Prospekt, hell bent on bumping into him and forcing him to acknowledge him.

The fear of stalking is a by-product of urban mass culture, and its roots can be traced through stories like *The Underground Man*, *Our Mutual Friend* and 'Man of the Crowd'. They show how the streets of the modern city provoke fantasies about 'the Other' – fantasies which are integral to stalking behaviour. The city teases out our ambivalent desires about our relationship to the strangers with whom we share our space. As I explained in the previous chapter, it is this ambivalence that provides the foundation for modern 'stalking culture'. Contemporary narcissistic existence is really a magnification of the basic elements of urban modernity as it emerged in the nineteenth century. To live in the modern world is like being a city-dweller in the crowded London streets described by the likes of Poe, Baudelaire, Dostoevsky and Dickens, subject to a flux of sensations of uncertainty, multiplicity and rapidity – only now the equivalent of the thronging streets is the vast network of mass media representations, and as well as other people, we are caught up in a vortex of media-generated images and narratives, ideological messages, and adverts. The 'double fantasy' produced by the experience of walking through crowded streets, in which an unknown other is either idealized or made into a threatening object, is even more prevalent when the crowdedness is not simply material. Consider how the multitude of celebrities who flit in and out of our lives as we flick through the channels or turn the pages of a newspaper or magazine will switch back and forth from appearing either unaccountably appealing or deeply, irrationally, irritating.

This extreme, double way of relating to the other person resembles the way objects figure in the unconscious in pathological narcissism, veering wildly between excessive admiration and extreme hostility. As Christopher Lasch's portrait of contemporary culture (mentioned in the previous chapter) accurately conveys, narcissism is not just about overvaluing oneself but feeling extreme hostility towards those who threaten our self-image. To my mind, Meloy's notion of the 'narcissistic linking fantasy' doesn't really make enough of this destructive element of narcissism. He characterizes it as involving, at a conscious level, positive scenarios of loving, idealizing, mirroring, complementing, merging, etc., which then go sour once rejection occurs. But stalking *also* involves unconscious fantasies of mastery, destruction and suffering. If the stalker's fantasy is narcissistic, then it means that, true to the logic of narcissism, it is ambivalent.

As Slavoj Žižek has argued, fantasy tends to be split into two co-dependent dimensions, linked like the two sides of a coin. On the one hand there is the '*stabilizing*' fantasy, something that emphasizes positive elements about the desired object, imagining a harmonious, mutually nourishing relationship with them. On the other, there is the '*destabilizing*' fantasy, which is the opposite. Its 'elementary form', Žižek says,

is envy. It encompasses all that "irritates" me about the Other, images that haunt me about what he or she is doing when out of my sight, about how he or she deceives me and plots against me, about how or she ignores me and indulges in an enjoyment that is intensive beyond my capacity of representation, etc.[17]

The two dimensions are neatly illustrated in *Our Mutual Friend*, where the obverse of Headstone's infatuation with Lizzie is his equally obsessive desire to eliminate Wrayburn, his exaggerated hatred supporting his idealistic love. But, more generally, this story and 'Man of the Crowd' suggest that this kind of 'double fantasy' is generated by city life.

The *Flâneur*

The stalker may not have begun to lurk in the public imagination until the end of the twentieth century, but there were plenty of 'dangerous individuals' stalking the nineteenth-century streets, from thieves and pickpockets, to garrotters, vitriol-throwers and murderers. But the character who seems most like a direct ancestor of the stalker was not really a criminal at all – perhaps he was not even *real*.

Poe's and Baudelaire's writings provide a portrait of a figure called the *flâneur*, the ultimate creature of the crowd. As Benjamin put it, '[t]he crowd is his element, as the air is that of birds and water of fishes. His passion and profession are to become one flesh with the crowd.'[18] While no doubt based on the real inhabitants of the nineteenth-century streets, such as the person who loafed around the new shopping arcades, the *flâneur* is probably a fictitious figure invented by cultural theorists like Benjamin to signify a kind of urban mobility and control which emerged in the mid nineteenth century. The *flâneur* was able to move anywhere he liked throughout the city and to see and *know* all. His special ability was to classify the passers-by on the city streets into categories. This is what the narrator of 'Man of the Crowd', the exemplary *flâneur*, is doing at the beginning of the story: determining from clothing and demeanour whether the people he watches are businessmen, clerks, pickpockets, gamblers, pedlars, etc. Though presented as a lover of the city and the crowd, the position of power the *flâneur* obviously enjoys over the others in the city (and the fact that historical conditions dictated he was likely to be a man)[19] means that there is potentially something rather suspect about him too.

But just as 'Man of the Crowd' offers a definitive illustration of the *flâneur*, so it also exposes his weakness – the limitations of his practice of categorization. What disturbs him about the old man he follows is that he is unable to classify him the way he can the others. This defeat, it has been argued, is a significant one in terms of literary genre, for it paves the way for the detective story. The detective effectively superseded the *flâneur* by harnessing his characteristics – blending in with the crowd while remaining detached, observing, decoding, categorizing – but, this time, directing them towards a sociologically valuable end: revealing the dark threatening secret at the heart of the crowd and thus alleviating fear. This is why Benjamin called 'Man of the Crowd' an x-ray of a detective story, for it presents the bare bones of a crime mystery, but as if incomplete, begging for the entry of a detective. Sure enough, in the years immediately following 'Man of the Crowd', Poe was to publish the three stories which are regarded as the first detective stories 'proper', featuring his mysterious *flâneur*-detective Dupin.

Another emergent investigative figure at this time was the journalist. From the 1830s to the 1850s, newspapers, which had been in existence in a more or less modern form since the seventeenth century, became truly big business. Mass circulation began of the 'penny papers' in London, a stream of New York papers such as the *Sun, Herald, Tribune* and the *New York Times*, and the Parisian *La Presse*. More significantly, the practice of 'waiting' for news to come via letter or first-hand account was eclipsed by the practice of 'reporting', where journalists would actually go out to gather news and report back. Both detective and journalist practise activities that we might describe as 'legitimate' stalking.

The similarity between the *flâneur* and his descendants the detective and the journalist point to his potential social value. But the fact remains that the *flâneur* is a complex, double figure, at once guardian against the unknown and also a potentially menacing figure himself. His sinister potential is suggested by Baudelaire's choice, at one point in his essay on the *flâneur*, of a hunting metaphor to describe urban life. The growth of the big cities, he says, prepared the ground for 'the most perfect of beasts of prey', man – a predator capable of 'grab[bing] his victim on a boulevard or stab[bing] his quarry in unknown woods'.[20] Benjamin interprets this as a reference to the atmosphere of ruthless competition which permeated city life and which, he thinks, served to puncture the illusion of the *flâneur*, but a literal interpretation is far from untenable – after all, the presence in the crowd of a whole range of dangerous individuals is the reason Benjamin suggests that the detective story comes into being. The predatory potential of the *flâneur* suggests a parallel with more unequivocally sinister figures like the prowler or the rapist, perhaps even the serial killer, another dangerous individual who emerges towards the end of the nineteenth century.[21]

Besides giving us a portrait of the prototypical detective, 'Man of the Crowd' also points to an undeniably dark side to the *flâneur*. It presents us not with one *flâneur*, but two – or to put it differently, the two figures in the story, follower and quarry, are blurred into one. Although it is the mysterious man rather than the narrator who is referred to explicitly as 'Man of the Crowd', the title retains a sense of ambiguity, for both figures are clearly 'men of the crowd'. This existential connection is emphasized in the language of compulsion used to describe both character's actions: e.g. the unknown man's 'mad energy' in retracing his steps to the centre of London at the end is matched by the narrator's 'wildest amazement' as he follows him there. The identification of the old man with 'deep crime' in the conclusion of the story, by implication, extends to the pursuer. Benjamin nicely underlines this ambiguity in his comment, 'No matter what trail the *flâneur* may follow, every one of them will lead to a crime'. If we see the *flâneur* as prototype detective this suggests that he has the ability to sniff out crime at every juncture. But if we acknowledge the sinister elements of the *flâneur* himself, it suggests that his activities themselves will inevitably result in crime.

From *Flâneur* to Stalker

Twentieth and twenty-first-century versions of the *flâneur* lean overwhelmingly towards this latter, more sinister, characterization. A large number of stories and films are built upon the same basic stalking structure as 'Man of the Crowd' – one person following another in the crowded modern city – and also seem to evoke the idea of the *flâneur*. But, just as in Poe, where the *flâneur*'s composure and self-control rapidly evaporates, it seems that, in modern reworkings, the *flâneur* is always on the verge of lapsing into psychopathology or crime.

Consider Thomas Mann's novella *Death in Venice* (1916), where the hero, Gustav von Aschenbach, begins as the very embodiment of the civilized European soul, strolling around Munich watching the crowds, but ends up feverishly and pathetically tracking Tadzio, the young boy he has become infatuated with, around Venice. Or *Taxi Driver*, sixty years later, where Bickle drifts invisibly through the New York nightlife – 'Not noticed, no reason to be noticed', 'at one with his surroundings' – spending his time classifying '[a]ll the animals [who] come out at night: whores, skunk pussies, buggers, queens, fairies, dopers, junkies, sick, venal', and able to stalk women from the safety of his cab – as we see him doing twice. His eponymous job is significant here: Bickle's cab is a more literal embodiment of the untouchable quality of the *flâneur*, and signals that we have moved from the densely populated streets of the nineteenth-century city to the tumultuous postmodern metropolis – from the man in the crowd to 'a man on the screen who's a fucking vehicle' (as Scorsese described the premise of his film).[22]

More recently there is Christopher Nolan's film *Following* (1999), both of whose two central characters – the young writer Bill and his nemesis Cobb, the cat-burglar – are like *flâneurs*, masters of the city they inhabit. In fact, the story in *Following* begins at the point where 'Man of the Crowd' leaves off. In Cobb Bill comes face to face with 'the type and genius of deep crime', but instead of leaving it there, the film proceeds to give us an insight into the exact nature of that crime. Appropriately enough, it is violent intrusion into another's life. Rather than searching the homes he enters for things he can sell, Cobb examines the objects inside for traces that can enable him to build up a picture of the owner. What he really steals from his victims is their private lives: 'You take it away and show them what they had.'

If the twentieth-century incarnation of the *flâneur* explicitly emphasizes his potential menace, a similar transformation marks how we perceive the apparently benign, reassuring figures he metamorphosed into in the nineteenth century, the detective and the journalist.

Naturally, as the point is to track down criminals, the detective genre has always been full of examples of stalking behaviour. The popular image of Sherlock Holmes in an upright crouching position, peering through a magnifying glass and wearing a deerstalker (which he never wore in the stories, but which emphasizes his cultural credentials as benign hunter-supreme) exemplifies this neatly. But, by and large, apart from some curious moments where the detective seems a little sinister, to say the least (we might think of Dupin's nocturnal wanderings, or Holmes's odd behaviour on the moor in *The Hound of the Baskervilles*, where he effectively stalks Watson) there can be no doubt that fictional detectives, for the first one hundred years of the genre, are essentially good, if eccentric, people, who act in the interests of society as a whole.

Yet twentieth-century crime fiction is full of detectives who lose their sense of perspective, and whose interest in the case seems to feed their desires or fantasies rather than fulfil their obligation to justice or their client. It is a blurring of roles summed up by the comment Sandy makes to the detective-surrogate in David Lynch's film *Blue Velvet* (1986): 'I don't know if you're a detective or a pervert.' Often a symptom of this perversion is when legitimate tailing procedures descend into inappropriate stalking behaviour. The classic cinematic example here is the extraordinary 20-minute sequence in Alfred Hitchcock's *Vertigo* (1958), where retired detective John 'Scottie' Ferguson (played by James Stewart) follows Madeleine everywhere she goes, tailing her in the car, tracking her on foot, shrinking back behind doors, peering out from behind gravestones, taking notes. The fact that he has lost all sense of detachment (if he ever had it) is underlined in the episode when Madeleine wakes up having been rescued by Scottie from the sea and taken home, apparently unconscious, where he has clearly undressed her before putting her to bed. The hint of an illicit thrill here, at taking advantage of someone, in fact points to the truth about their whole relationship – and indeed the film as a whole.

Similarly warped investigations abound in prose fiction. Paul Auster's *City of Glass* (1985), for example, features a detective figure who is so determined not to lose sight of the suspect he is tailing that he eventually abandons his home and camps out in the street near his apartment, sleeping in garbage cans until, starved to the point of death, he descends into delirium. Marc Behm's novel *The Eye of the Beholder* (1980) takes the idea of detective-as-stalker to its furthest point. It begins conventionally for a 'hard-boiled' detective novel when a disaffected detective – known only as 'The Eye' – is called in to investigate a mysterious disappearance. He soon finds his quarry, a young man called Paul Hugo who has run off with a girlfriend, Joanna Eris. The Eye observes them get married and then tails them to a house, where, hiding in the dark outside, the Eye witnesses Joanna murder Paul and steal his money. But rather than arrest or report her the Eye continues to follow her, each time installing himself in secret outside her window and watching as she commits similar crimes over and over again.

Obviously 'The Eye' is seriously disturbed, perhaps even sociopathic, himself. But his name universalizes him. It is clearly a short form of the euphemistic term for 'Private Investigator', the 'private eye', the detective who works independently but whose special ability is also to *see* what others miss. The term was coined after the establishment of the Pinkerton's detective agency in 1852, whose motto was 'We Never Sleep' and whose corporate logo was a picture of a watchful eye. *The Eye of the Beholder* shows how the standard activities of the detective can service psychopathological ends. The Eye's continual voyeurism is a parody of surveillance. Recording her movements and writing reports is a symptom of his obsession with Joanna, but resemble the legitimate activities of the policeman. Even the disturbing scene when he dresses up as a nanny and pushes a pram past the house in which Joanna is staying, pretending 'the empty bundle' in the buggy is his lost daughter, amounts to the principle of disguise and the dedication of the pursuer taken to psychotic extremes, until the role he is playing comes to take him over completely. Overall the book suggests that the detective's activities are on the edge of what is permissible itself: breaking and entering, or prowling outside a house, are acceptable when the endpoint is justice, but it is easy for the line to be crossed. Maintaining the law, the book implies, entails breaking it. The novel is a natural product of a time when our faith in the authority of the law is in crisis.

Besides detection, the other great investigative profession instituted in the mid nineteenth century becomes subject to a kind of perversion in the late twentieth century, as the news reporter metamorphosed into the paparazzo. Susan Sontag described the photographer equipped with his weapon, the camera, as 'an extension of the eye of the middle-class *flâneur*'.[23] A thriller of the time, 1978's *The Eyes of Laura Mars*, offers a dramatic way of considering the implications of the relationship between stalking and photography. It tells the story of a famous photographer, Laura Mars, whose models are being murdered serially by an unknown man, who eventually turns out to be her lover. The film's principal conceit is that Mars experiences visions of precisely what the killer can see as he stalks and kills his victims. Though she is not the murderer, these visions mean that she is complicit in the murders. Thus the parallel between her profession, which involves 'capturing' models, and the gruesome practice of her lover, is made clear. Significantly, the film was made at the time when the word stalking was beginning to feature in the media in relation both to the paparazzi and serial killers.

The association between 'stalking' and photography is an enduring one. In the voiceover to a more recent film, *One Hour Photo*, Sy Parrish explains that the term 'snapshot' originally (in 1808) related to hunting. As much as it is a device to record domestic happiness, the camera is also to be envisaged as an instrument of invasion, something that facilitates the invasive practices of the stalker. These opposed functions of the snapshot are central to Parrish's story. While he carries photographs of the Yorkins so he can pretend they're his own family, and imagines that a photo of him is on their fridge, he also ends up punishing David Yorkin and his lover for their adultery, by forcing them to act out pornographic scenes at knifepoint, captured on camera – just as Parrish's abusive father forced him to pose for degrading snapshots as a child.

The way this film dwells on the sinister capacity of the snapshot, its seeming unwillingness to stick with the innocent use of the family photograph, is typical of the way twentieth-century culture apparently cannot help but focus on the dark side of an activity – walking in the city, detection, photography. In the time that has elapsed between Poe's 'Man of the Crowd' and *One Hour Photo* culture has been shaped by a thoroughly post-Freudian awareness that normal behaviour is never far from lapsing into pathology, that comfortable everyday existence is under perennial threat from violent crime. That the pathology is there at the very inception of our modern world is abundantly clear from the compulsive behaviour depicted in texts like 'Man of the Crowd' and *Our Mutual Friend*. Now, though, in the age of the stalker, it seems that the relationship between the normal and the pathological or criminal is fatally overbalanced by the latter.

From the beginning of the nineteenth century to the late 1980s and early 1990s stalking moves from the cultural unconscious, where it is a submerged recognition of something that might occur in the modern city, to the cultural consciousness, where, supported by formal classification from psychiatry and the law, it is recognized as a very real danger to anyone who lives in the modern world. The crucial period in this transition is from around 1961 to 1989 (that is, from the publication of the *Time* article about the paparazzi to Robert Bardo's murder of Rebecca Schaeffer) when stalking is neither criminalized nor pathologized, but is clearly 'bubbling under' in the cultural mind. It is in this period that we find *flâneur*-stalkers like Travis Bickle in *Taxi Driver*, or Vito Acconci in his work of performance art, *Following Piece* (1969). In this period we also encounter figures who are stripped of the *flâneur*'s interest in the city or the crowd, but who retain a fascination with another person – only this time seeking systematically to destroy him. One incarnation is to be found in 'slasher' or 'stalker' movies such as *The Texas Chainsaw Massacre* (1974) and *Halloween* (1978), a deranged killer who stalks and kills one by one a group of teenagers. Another is the anonymous truckdriver in Steven Spielberg's terrifying depiction of 'road rage', *Duel* (1971).

More than any other, this film begs to be read as a disguised update of 'Man of the Crowd', because, like Poe's story, it strips the stalking paradigm down to its basic choreography. Having tried to overtake a large diesel truck hogging the road while driving through a remote part of California on his way to a business appointment, David Mann is pursued and harassed relentlessly by the truck for the rest of his journey. As we never see the driver (except for his forearms at the wheel and his cowboy boots) we are never given an insight into his motivations, and have to assume that he is a psychopath roused to aggression by spite. Nevertheless the basics of a stalking case are there: the perceived slight, the relentless, hostile pursuit, the clever setting of traps, the effect of causing the victim to feel that the aggressor is all-powerful and everywhere.

But most interesting about *Duel* is the way it elevates the basic stalking paradigm to serve as a commentary on the hostile nature of the modern existence. As the emblematic surname of the central character indicates, he represents modern man, alone in the world engaged in a struggle with the Other. Life is thus presented as unremittingly bleak, a constant struggle between self and other. It is fitting that all we know about David Mann is that he is on a business trip, for business in the late-capitalist universe signifies competition, the elimination of one's rival. It is also significant that many of the other characters in the film are slightly sinister and potentially hostile themselves; they refuse to get involved or assume that Mann is crazy. *Duel* lives up to what the earliest 'modern' stalking stories such as 'Man of the Crowd' and *Our Mutual Friend* predict. Stalking as we conceive of it now is a product of the paranoid, narcissistic universe of modernity, where we fear we are subject to being accosted by a hostile stranger at any moment.

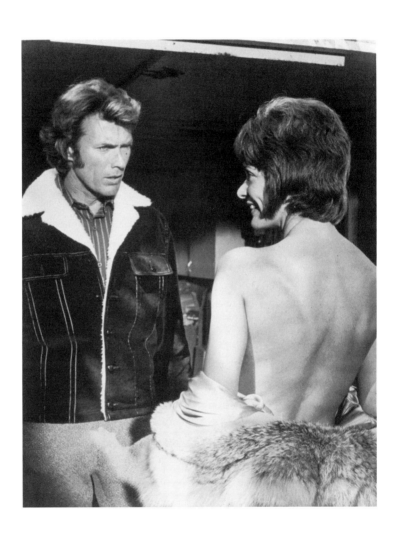

CHAPTER FOUR

Stalking and Love

Then Terri said: 'He beat me up one night. He dragged me around the living
room by my ankles. He kept saying, "I love you, I love you, you bitch". He went
on dragging me around the living room. My head kept knocking on things'.
Terri looked around the table: 'What do you do with love like that?'

Raymond Carver, 'What We Talk about When We Talk about Love' (1981)

What *do* we talk about when we talk about love? Raymond Carver's story
makes you wonder, for it contrasts the different kinds of relationship we term
'love'. The main opposition is between the kind of love enjoyed by his characters Nick and Laura who are 'in love', and are also companions, and the
kind of love Terri had to endure at the hands of her ex-husband, Ed. He used
to beat her, and then when she left him, harassed her new partner, Mel.
Eventually Ed shot himself. To Mel's extreme irritation Terri maintains that,
as painful as it was to experience, it was still love: 'Sure, it's abnormal in most
people's eyes. But he was willing to die for it.'[1]

The fact that stalking complicates our ideas of what is 'normal' has
seldom been far from our concern in this book. Stalking can be explained

101

by the 'narcissistic linking fantasy' – but, as we have seen, to an extent this is a *normal*, even idealized, dimension of human attachment, especially in modern celebrity-obsessed culture. It is considered acceptable that fans are obsessed by a particular band or football team, or that people should regularly peek into the lives of celebrities in the pages of *Hello!* or *Heat* magazine. Both impulses, though – as films like *The King of Comedy* and *The Fan* show – can lead to stalking behaviour. We respect detective-work and even invasive journalism as 'legitimate' stalking behaviour because they are conducted in the name of 'justice' or the 'public interest'. Yet films and books such as *Vertigo* and *The Eye of the Beholder* demonstrate that it's but a short step for this line to be crossed.

Most of all, stalking culture asks uncomfortable questions about what ought to be deemed normal – or otherwise – when it comes to love. 'Love' is a word we use all the time, to refer (as the couples in Carver's story do) to a bewildering variety of different kinds of attachment between one person and another: carnal, spiritual, obsessive, violent, platonic, parental, etc. Yet despite this, despite its importance to our lives, we tend to take it for granted. One effect of stalking is that, for those who come into contact with it – either as victims, or as viewers of films or readers of books or newspaper stories – is to 'defamiliarize' love and make them think again about what it means.

More than any other crime, except perhaps what the French call the '*le crime passionnel*', stalking is motivated by love. The two main categories of stalking where ordinary people are victims – 'former intimacy' and 'desired intimacy' – are both about romantic relationships which have 'gone sour', are desired or mistakenly imagined. Celebrity stalking, too, typically revolves around a desperate form of intimacy-seeking – manifested either in the delusion that the celebrity is in love with the stalker, or that the celebrity might be seduced into a reciprocal affair. A common conceit amongst celebrity stalkers is the conviction of being the spouse of the victim. Perhaps the most infamous example is David Letterman's stalker

Margaret Ray, who, when apprehended after stealing his Porsche and failing to pay the $3 toll at the Lincoln Tunnel in New York, informed police she was his wife and the mother of their child. Also commonly cherished by stalkers is the notion of *ideal* love. Arthur Jackson, the man who pursued and stabbed the actress Theresa Saldana in 1982, explained in his diary that he had 'psychedelic fantasies of romance about her in springtime – enchanting visions of our walking together through the gardens of magnificent palaces in Heaven'.[2]

Stalking cases often appear like grotesque parodies of love affairs, with both parties unable to avoid thinking about each other. Often the material sent by stalkers to their victims could be mistaken for communications between lovers. Take John W. Hinckley's letters to Jodie Foster, for example. The opening paragraph of one implores the actress humbly, passionately, to accept his love: 'As you well know by now I love you very much. Over the past seven months I've left you dozens of poems, letters and love messages in the faint hope that you could develop an interest in me. Although we talked on the phone a couple of times I never had the nerve to simply approach you and introduce myself.' In isolation this passage seems like a typical love letter – until we take into account its chilling opening statement that '[t]here is definitely a possibility that I will be killed in my attempt to get Reagan'.[3] Robert Fine found that the affidavit prepared by his stalker alleging he harassed her, 'often read like an old-fashioned romance in which the male hero fixes on the heroine "with a hard stare which almost seemed to pierce into her."'[4]

Erotomania

These examples remind us that although stalking is motivated by love, and although it highlights the problems with determining what is normal or otherwise in love, it is often motivated by a dangerous inability to distinguish the real from the unreal. Clinically speaking, stalkers are very often *delusional*, and this side of their nature is often most visible in their attitudes to love. In particular they nurse one particular sustained, systematic delusion about their relationship with another person.

What is notable about delusional disorders is that they cannot be dispelled by psychotherapy, no matter how rigorous, nor by being confronted with 'the facts', no matter how forcefully or patiently. Many victims of stalking become painfully aware of this. It is another explanation for the extraordinary longevity of the obsessions which motivate stalking, conveyed in painful detail in memoirs by stalking-victims such as *Being Stalked* by Robert Fine or Doreen Orion's *I Know You Really Love Me*, where the persecution looks like it will never end. But, more precisely, stalkers tend to suffer from a particularly deceptive kind of delusion.

Psychoanalysis distinguishes between two main kinds of delusion. The most obvious type is associated with schizophrenia. Because this is the kind of belief that is obviously at odds with reality and is held by someone who is obviously in a confused and distressed state, it is quite easy to tell when someone is subject to it. An example is Daniel Paul Schreber, whose memoir detailing his paranoid schizophrenia, *Memoirs of my Nervous Illness* (1903), was analysed by Freud in 1911. Schreber was convinced God was systematically transforming him into a woman by sending down 'rays' which would enable Him to violate Schreber sexually and thereby produce a new human race.

Many stalkers are subject to similarly outlandish delusions. Arthur Jackson, for example, believed that God wanted him 'united in heaven' with Theresa Saldana. He therefore planned to kill her so that he would be executed and join her in death. Günther Parche, the man who stabbed the tennis player Monica Seles on court in 1993 because he wanted to help the woman he was stalking, Steffi Graf, regain the number 1 spot in the rankings, claimed that he was Seles's real father, as his sperm had been used in a CIA experiment to produce professional athletes.[5] But such extreme examples are in fact rare. Stalkers are not schizophrenics. They rarely suffer from psychotic delusions, nor do they often display associated symptoms, like hallucinations and disorganized thought or speech.

More frequently stalkers, especially those who refuse to accept that a relationship is over, are beset by a kind of delusion that is less easy to identify and which doesn't obviously seem the product of mental illness. This type of delusion is associated with 'paranoid thought disorder'. It is more insidious and less easy to shake because it depends upon an apparently rational logic. According to Pierre Bayard, what is distinctive about paranoid thought disorder is the fact that 'it offers all the seductions of a reasoned discourse'. It is characterized by what he calls its 'false coherence', the way that, on the surface, all the facts of the 'case' fit together according to established laws of causality, even though they 'are entirely dependent on the solution they are enlisted to serve'.[6]

The most extreme kind of delusional state associated with stalking falls somewhere between the two – outright schizophrenia and paranoid thought disorder – and is undoubtedly one of the strangest pathological phenomena there is: erotomania, the condition where the sufferer is absolutely convinced that someone is in love with them, despite all evidence to the contrary. Modern understandings of the phenomenon date back to 1942, when the psychiatrist Gaétan Gatian de Clérambault claimed that he had isolated a 'pure' form of the condition, where the erotomania is the 'totality of the clinical picture' and there are no other psychotic symptoms.[7] This became known as de Clérambault's syndrome (though he himself called it *psychose passionelle*). Its 'fundamental postulate', he claimed, was the 'conviction of being in amorous communication with a person of much higher rank, who has been the first to fall in love and was the first to make advances'.[8] Clérambault provided five detailed case studies of erotomaniacs in his book *Les Psychoses passionelles* (1942) – each of which might be regarded as documents of stalking cases, since the subject's attentions were unwanted and they involved constant, escalating patterns of persecution. The most famous one is the example of the 53-year-old woman who was convinced that King George V was in love with her, despite no supporting evidence whatsoever. She would wait continuously outside Buckingham Palace (where she 'once saw a curtain move in one of the palace windows and interpreted this as a signal from the King'), and was convinced that the King was preventing her from finding accommodation in London and had secretly arranged that she lose her luggage.[9]

Nowadays psychiatrists are unsure whether 'pure' erotomania exists, and also dispute de Clérambault's insistence that erotomania begins with a precise and sudden onset. If it exists, pure erotomania does not just erupt out of nothing. The erotomaniac is likely to be 'a socially inept individual isolated from others, be it by sensitivity, suspiciousness, or assumed superiority'. More recent studies of people who have succumbed to the disorder found them to be deeply narcissistic, characterized by 'an exquisite self-consciousness and tendency to refer the slightest actions or utterances of others to themselves, usually endowing them with a denigratory or malevolent colouring'.[10] This extreme, paranoid sensitivity means that when the actions or utterances of a specific person do *not* seem to fit this pattern, but seem on the contrary benign, even loving, then it is likely to prove a radical shock to the system. Just as insignificant indifferent gestures are erroneously assumed to be hostile, so mildly caring gestures will be overinterpreted as excessive love.

The basic erotomanic scenario is encapsulated by George Herriman's 'Krazy Kat' series of comic strips, which ran from around 1900 to 1930. Krazy Kat is in love with Ignatz Mouse and pursues him despite Ignatz's continued violent rejection of him, usually by hurling bricks at Krazy Kat's head. But – and this is the aspect which makes it a case of erotomania – Krazy Kat always sees each rejection as further evidence of Ignatz's undoubted love for him. The delusion illustrates the kind of 'vortex of interpretation' typical of erotomania, and is another example of the circular logic that typifies stalking. To enter into any kind of dialogue or exchange with the stalker fuels their stalking behaviour. The trouble is, though, that it is impossible *not* to enter into a kind of 'dialogue', since even not responding will be regarded as a response. Every event, every response, not matter how incontrovertibly they might seem to contradict the erotomaniac's delusion, becomes absorbed into it, making it even stronger. A good example of this is the case of the woman who screamed at her erotomanic stalker to 'fuck off', only for him to treat it as evidence of their increasing intimacy. After all, he reasoned, isn't fucking an aspect of love?[11]

Erotomania's capacity to transform anything that threatens its logic into support for it is something that is powerfully conveyed by depictions of deluded lovers in the contemporary novel, e.g. Patricia Highsmith's novel *This Sweet Sickness* (1960) or Iris Murdoch's *The Sea, the Sea* (1978), perhaps because the novel is the art-form which excels at detailing what goes on in the individual mind. The heroes of both these novels manage skilfully to turn anything that would seem to contradict their perception of events into further support for it. When Annabelle tells Highsmith's anti-hero David Kelsey straight that she doesn't want to divorce her husband and move in with him, for example, he 'realizes' that 'Annabelle might *think* she meant what she said' but is fooling herself because she is so determined to make it work out with a husband who is unsuited to her.[12]

But we mustn't assume that erotomaniacs gain a simple pleasure from their interpretive gymnastics. In fact, their delusional logic means that the sufferer regards the love object's actions as upsettingly contradictory or paradoxical. They commonly think, 'my beloved may appear to hate me and want to harm me, but really s/he loves me'. This is how the erotomaniac can account for things that they cannot deny really happened but that appear to contradict their beliefs. It reminds us of the unhappy fact that with stalking cases we are really dealing with two victims rather than just one, not just the object of the stalking course of conduct, but its perpetrator (a recognition which is now at the heart of programmes of psychiatric treatment for those involved in stalking cases).

Erotomania makes the distinctive mirroring-effect of stalking particularly stark: the erotomaniac's actions are driven by paranoid convictions, which eventually become delusions of persecution, while the victim quickly descends into a state of paranoia as a result of *real* persecution at the hands of the stalker. Cases of erotomania typically last for years, longer than other kinds of stalking. Despite the constancy of their emotions and the resilience of the delusion, continued rejection can make the erotomaniac resentful or hateful. This is when erotomania can become dangerous. De Clérambault insisted that erotomania was rooted not in love but in *sexual pride*: 'pride predominates over passion, for never has thwarted passion been able to produce such durable results'.[13] In other words, only something as stubborn as pride could ensure such persistence in the face of such consistent rejection. Sexual desire is fickle by comparison.

Erotomania is proof, if further proof were needed, that stalking is an old behaviour (but a new crime). But what's also interesting about it is the way the condition reflects cultural assumptions about normal and abnormal forms of love. The conflict between these inspired Ian McEwan's novel about erotomania, *Enduring Love*. Experiencing (or enduring – the title is of course double) Jed Parry's abnormal love, Joe Rose is caused to reflect upon why his 'normal' relationship with his partner Clarissa is going wrong. As he put it, '[f]or there to be a pathology there had to be a lurking concept of health. De Clérambault's syndrome was a dark, distorting mirror that reflected and parodied a brighter world of lovers whose reckless abandon to their cause was sane.'[14]

Erotomania wasn't discovered by de Clérambault, but is a disorder referred to in medical discourse as far back as classical Greece.[15] What is consistent about all the references is that the condition has almost always been treated as a *pathological* form of love. By the early nineteenth century, the condition had become criminalized, too. In 1840 – the same year as Poe's 'Man of the Crowd' – the French medical theorist D. A. Portemer argued that the erotomaniac, under the grip of his obsession, 'is prone to commit criminal acts ranging from theft to physical attacks on or murder of his lover or any rival'.[16]

The association between erotomania and crime coincides with the rise of psychiatry throughout the nineteenth century. This had a profound influence on the function of the law, according to Foucault. Rather than dispensing justice, the legal apparatus saw itself as a mechanism for 'public hygiene', with a duty to cleanse the social body of its pathological elements. To do this involved a strategy Foucault terms the 'dividing practice',[17] a method by which people could be separated into subdivisions of the 'normal' and the 'abnormal'. In the courts, this meant marking off the criminals from the non-criminals; in hospitals, the healthy from the sick; and in psychiatric clinics, the sane from the mad. The strategy involved building up an overall picture of the normal social being – one who was healthy, sane, law-abiding, etc. – according to which deviants, those who did not resemble the portrait, could easily be identified and isolated. But the irony, which fascinated Foucault, is that the procedure doesn't really involve *measuring* deviations against the norm, it actually *creates* them. Once you try to impose limits on anything as diverse as humanity and society, there will always be exceptions.

Throughout the nineteenth century, erotomania became subject to this process, so that by the time we reach the renewed interest in the phenomenon in the twentieth century, sparked by the work of de Clérambault, erotomania figures as a deviation from the norm of love. If the abnormal lover is one who persists in amorous feelings and actions despite a clear rejection from the object of his or her love, it follows that the 'normal' lover seeks a love that is *mutual*, in which both partners reciprocate. This is why Gregory Dart simply equates stalking with 'unrequited love' in his memoir of that title.

'Romantic Love' and Stalking

Dart's decision is reasonable. But to assume that 'normal' love is therefore free of delusion or narcissism, even from a degree of harassment or violence, is not necessarily as commonsensical as it seems. Stalkers may be delusional but the fact is that the subject they are deluded about, namely love, is by no means a straightforward one in contemporary culture. What we talk about when we talk about love in contemporary society, more often than not, is influenced by one particular ideology of love which has dominated modern western culture since the late eighteenth century and still functions today: 'romantic love'. Romantic love is defined as 'any intense attraction involving the idealization of the other within an erotic context. The idealization carries with it the desire for intimacy and the pleasurable expectation of enduring for some unknown time into the future.'[18] It is more than just sexual desire. Equally it is more than non-sexual, or 'Platonic' love. It operates as a set of conventions which structure the thousands of love stories in modern literature and film, but also shape our everyday attitudes about what love is and ought to be.

Three themes recur continually in the discourse of romantic love which are relevant to stalking. First, love is idealized as something long-lasting, if not eternal, something that can endure – as it seems to in romantic novels such as *Wuthering Heights* – beyond the grave. Second, love is envisaged as a powerful force that is beyond our control, that can push us off balance in our ordinary lives, making us behave 'madly' or as if (love)sick. Its onset is unforeseen and shocking. Third, because of this extreme other-worldly power, romantic love is imagined as a force which demands persistence on the part of those who succumb to it – especially men. Mutual, reciprocal love is certainly an ideal in the conventions of romantic love, but it is never more than an option. Whether a lover's passion is requited or not has little bearing on the validity of his love. If it hurts, it's real. (This is, after all, what unrequited love is all about.) Romantic love doesn't envisage love as straightforwardly pleasurable or fulfilling, for built in to the concept is a masochistic idea of pleasure-in-suffering.

These kinds of attitudes obviously clash with the liberal-democratic values which prevail in modern Western society, which state that we are more or less free to do anything we like so long as we don't hurt another person. Stalking highlights the incompatibility of these two ideologies – romantic love versus liberal democracy – especially starkly. Social codes make it clear that someone must not harass another person, nor violate their rights or private space. Yet social existence is underpinned by a cultural world, a torrent of stories, films, TV programmes, adverts, newspaper articles, that perpetuate the ideals of romantic love. Love, culture says, is eternal, violent, persistent. This means we cannot easily dismiss stalkers as people who are simply unable to adhere to the codes surrounding romantic relations in modern society the way 'the rest of us' do. There is undoubtedly something abnormal about their *actions*, which do separate them from the norm, but determining what is normal or abnormal about love is no straightforward matter.

Popular culture is packed with examples where obsessive and potentially disturbing behaviour is understood as a measure of real love – or, *vice versa*, when 'genuine' love is mistaken for unacceptable harassment. The confusion is most obvious when we consider pop songs. The 1983 Police record 'Every Breath You Take' is often misconceived as a beautiful heartfelt love song, when in fact it is a sinister tale of infatuation. 'Every breath you take / Every move you make / Every bond you break / Every step you take / I'll be watching you . . . Oh can't you see / You belong to me?' This is why it has been used as the title for numerous stalking thrillers or studies of stalking.[19] Another example is 'You Spin Me Round (Like A Record)', recorded in 1984 by Dead or Alive. This is often seen as a upbeat song about the pleasures of being head over heels in love. Closer inspection, however, reveals its credentials as a stalker's anthem. It begins with 'Yeah I,

I got to know your name / Well and I, could trace your private number baby' and then moves to 'I, I got to be your friend now baby / And I would like to move in'. The chorus is heralded by the cry 'Watch out, here I come!' The song is sung at the start of the comedy romance, *The Wedding Singer* (1998), apparently without irony, by its eponymous hero Robbie Hart, who finds 'real' love in the film. Somewhat more appropriately, it also features in the 2000 film adaptation of Bret Easton Ellis's serial-killer novel *American Psycho*.

Elsewhere in popular culture, the obverse conflation is made: love is mistaken for stalking. The British media response to recent airings of the 'reality TV' game-show *Big Brother* makes this clear. In the fifth series of the British version in 2004, the contestant Michelle Bass was widely referred to as a 'bunny-boiler' in the tabloid press because of the way she jealously protected her right to intimacy with her lover Stuart Wilson from other housemates. Viewers might otherwise have assumed that the intensity of her emotions were simply typical of someone in their early twenties experiencing 'real' love, perhaps for the first time. Similarly, in *Big Brother 6*, in 2005, homosexual Craig Coates's obvious distress at his unrequited love for heterosexual Anthony Hutton and his inability to leave him alone (a not unexpected kind of behaviour in such a confined space) led to him being labelled a 'paranoid stalker' by the tabloids. Tabloid media culture frequently assumes that excessive emotion must be threatening.

The problem, as psychologists have recognized, is that stalking takes place in a culture where love stories frequently imply that the more obsessive and determined a lover is, the more genuine and laudable are his sentiments. Literature and film continually place an emphasis on what the psychologist Glen Skoler calls 'violent attachment': from Dante's Beatrice to modern novels and films such as Marquez's *Love in the Time of Cholera* or *Il Postino*.[20] Doris M. Hall notes the popularity of films like *Indecent Proposal* or *The Piano*, in which a woman is not interested in a man until his persistence wins her over.[21] This attitude to obsessional pursuit, says J. Reid Meloy, effectively 'sanctions' stalking behaviour. While being shocked at the activities of stalkers, we sympathize with Carmen's murderer, laugh at the way that Charlie Brown's sister Sally pursues Linus in *Snoopy*, and wear Obsession perfume.[22]

One of the best examples of this process is Mike Nichols's 1967 film version of Charles Webb's novel *The Graduate*, widely regarded as one of the great modern love stories. After Elaine Robinson initially rejects him, Benjamin Braddock takes to driving past her house, watching her from behind bushes and writing her name endlessly on a piece of paper. When she leaves for university, he follows her and continues to watch her from behind trees and café windows, running across campus when he is about to lose sight of her. He takes a room nearby so he can devote himself to pursuing her full-time. He sits in on the lectures she attends. He engineers a meeting with her on a bus, and insists on accompanying her as she goes to meet her boyfriend, Carl, whom he is rude to. The famous end to the film sees him frantically tracking her down at her wedding to Carl, interrupting the ceremony, and the two eloping together.

It is one of the most joyous endings in cinema, its message a staple of romantic love: true love will win out in the end. Braddock's behaviour shows how fine the line is between acceptable and unacceptable behaviour in love. Because Elaine returns his love, his expressions of 'violent attachment' are regarded as permissible. It proves that what he was up to cannot have been stalking, for all along he was correct in his assumption that eventually she would say yes – even though she had in fact clearly and unequivocally said no to practically all of his demands throughout the film. The point here is not to somehow recast *The Graduate* as a stalking movie that we once naïvely took to be a love story, the way we need to with songs like 'Every Breath You Take' and 'You Spin Me Round'. It can never be anything other than a love story – and stalking can only properly be seen as stalking (in the eyes of the law or according to moral values) when there is a victim. Yet the message of *The Graduate* is clearly that true love sometimes requires persistence, if not more extreme persuasion. And this is a message which can clearly lead to disturbing consequences if received in the wrong way, say by a person predisposed to stalking behaviour.

It's clear that the notion of romantic love which operates so insistently in our society, and which underpins so many examples of popular culture, plays a significant part in shaping stalking behaviour. The universal awareness of its conventions also means that it contributes to the difficulty victims have in responding to a stalker's attentions in the early stages of his harassment. At first it may be remarkable to find that you have prompted such violent passions in another person. Because of the value our culture attaches to passionate love, it is natural to try to deal with someone confessing their love to you by letting them down gently, to say 'I don't feel ready to have a relationship with you just now' instead of what you mean: 'under any circumstances I do not and will not want to have any kind of relationship with you'. In *Enduring Love* it occurs to Rose during one of Parry's early efforts to persuade him that their love *is* mutual, Rose is amazed at

> how easy it was not to say, *Who the fuck are you? What are you talking about?* The language Parry was using set responses in me, old emotional sub-routines. It took an act of will to dismiss the sense that I owed this man, that I was being unreasonable in holding something back. In part, I was playing along with this domestic drama . . . [23]

So ingrained in our cultural memory are the conventions of love that they work as a kind of narrative template that everyone has instinctively mastered and which is difficult *not* to impose upon our experience of close relationships.

So our reaction to many pop culture products (songs, *Big Brother*, Hollywood films, etc.) blur the boundaries between legitimate and illegitimate obsessive pursuit unintentionally. Yet some stalking films much more consciously and cleverly set the two against each other, so that viewers are led to question what love is and ought to be. One way of looking at *Play Misty For Me* is as a terrifying thriller. But we could alternatively see it as a warped love story. Jessica Walter, who played Evelyn Draper, once said that she never thought of the film as a horror story but as 'a very intense love story'. The film contains a network of textual allusion that ironically questions the conventions of romantic love. Early versions of the film's publicity poster quoted lines from Elizabeth Barrett Browning's sonnet XLIII 'How do I love thee? Let me count the ways' and the familiar marriage vow, 'till death do us part'. Evelyn Draper quotes from Edgar Allan Poe's poem 'Annabel Lee'. The soundtrack features the song 'The First Time Ever I Saw Your Face' by Ewan MacColl. Each of these texts envisages a love so excessively strong that it survives after death – just like Draper's, in fact. But because Draper's love is revealed as destructive it causes us to question the assumption that the excess of 'normal' romantic love is valuable.

A more recent film, Miguel Arteta's *Chuck and Buck* (2000), provides an interesting reversal to the pattern adhered to by stalking texts like *Enduring Love* and *Play Misty For Me*. Here, stalking isn't presented ironically as love, love is initially depicted as stalking. Buck and Chuck (now known as Charlie) were childhood friends who have now met again by chance as adults. Though Charlie is clearly lukewarm about resuming their friendship, Buck, a rather emotionally retarded man, entirely unable to play the adult social game, plagues him with visits to his office and home. He is obviously in love with Charlie, and assumes their childhood relationship can continue precisely where it must have left off. Buck tells Charlie's fiancée about the 'sex things' he and Charlie did as children.

The film is a comment on how generic the stalking motif has become in Hollywood cinema. It plays on our instinctive recognition of the conventions of stalking movies, from proper 'studies of stalking' like *Play Misty For Me* to horror stories like *Dracula* or slasher movies like *Halloween*. On first viewing, there is something sinister about Buck's childlike obsession with Charlie, his inability to register Charlie's discomfort at the embarrassing things he says to his friends and partner. We fear that something dreadful is inevitably going to happen. The comic, playful feel to the movie, underlined by its bubblegum-pop soundtrack, appears to be an ironic way of disguising this underlying darkness. But on second viewing the film is radically changed because of the ending. Buck follows Charlie to a bar when, now openly hostile towards Buck, he agrees – foolishly, it seems – to spend one night with him back at Buck's apartment, on condition that Buck will then disappear from his life. At this point the suspense is at its height and we expect the intimations of doom to be fulfilled. But the twist is that Buck and Charlie end up sleeping together. Charlie confesses that he remembers everything. Buck is thereby vindicated: what they once shared *was* love. Buck's apparent emotional retardation is in fact an affirmation of the emotional authenticity of childhood. At this point we realize that the film's title has been an obvious clue, staring us in the face: they are *still* 'Chuck and Buck', they always have been.

So rather than a stalking story which skirts uncomfortably close to being a love story, *Chuck and Buck* is the opposite. Like *The Graduate*, what prevents the film from being a story of stalking is because the attraction is, ultimately, mutual. And this reminds us that for all the emphasis on forcefully winning someone over in Hollywood, most 'normal' people, those not subject to paranoid thought disorder, recognize the distinction between what we see in the movies and what you can get away with in real life. A headline in the online satirical news-magazine *The Onion* nicely sums up this awareness: 'Romantic-Comedy Behavior Gets Real-Life Man Arrested'.[24]

Stalking and Seduction

The exception that proves the rule is the remarkable example of ex-Abba singer, Agnetha Fältskog, who in 1997 began a relationship with her stalker.

Gert van der Graaf had given up his job in Holland and moved to Ekerö in Sweden, where Fältskog lived, and they began a relationship. Inevitably, after two years, the relationship soured, and van der Graaf then began to stalk her for a number of months until he was expelled from Sweden and forbidden to return for two years (though as soon as the period was up, he went straight back only to be expelled and banned once more). Fältskog explained later, 'It was an extremely intensive courtship from his side, I could no longer resist, I wanted to get to know him. We began a relationship despite the fact that I saw that he was an odd person.'[25]

Her reference to an intense *courtship* here is significant. For although we might consider the distinction between obsessive pursuit and stalking as a simple equation, 'pursuit + acceptance = love' but 'pursuit + rejection + pursuit = stalking', the mechanics of *seduction*, the process arguably at the heart of the majority of love affairs, makes it more complex. If the acquiescence of the beloved means we cannot call what happens in, say, *The Graduate* stalking, then where does this place the more subtle but still often prolonged and relentless form of persuasion we call seduction – which is nothing less than the formalized mechanism of persistence in love? Considering the age-old art of seduction in the light of what we now know about stalking complicates the question of acceptable and unacceptable expressions of love still further.

'Seduction' derives from the Latin *se-* (aside, away) and *ducere* (to lead): to seduce is to lead astray or away from. Originally the term applied to persuading someone to transfer their allegiance; it began to be used in a specifically sexual sense only from 1560. The philosopher Jean Baudrillard argues that sexual seduction is really an aspect of a more fundamental law underlying the relationships between human beings that has been in operation since the Renaissance period. Seduction is, 'like politeness, or court manners – a conventional, aristocratic form, a game of strategy without any special connection to love'.[26] The 'game' involves making someone (i.e. the seduced person) aware of their obligation to another individual (i.e. the seducer) – not simply in terms of one-upmanship, but of developing and prolonging social interaction.

The kind of leading astray involved in seduction has nothing to do with coercion or force, nor with direct persuasion or enticement, for such crude efforts would only ensure that the object of persuasion becomes suspicious about what is being asked of them. Rather, to seduce someone successfully requires the almost paradoxical achievement of leading them astray by making them act *of their own free will*. The game is exemplified, Baudrillard argues, in a work by the conceptual artist Sophie Calle called *The Sleepers*, in which she invited 28 people to sleep one by one in her bed for eight hours while she watched them, photographed them every hour, and made notes. What fascinated Baudrillard about this is the fact that never, not once, did Calle meet with any refusal from the people she asked. This, he thinks, is precisely because of the very mystery and absurdity of her challenge. If she'd asked something reasonable and explicit of them (such as to fill out a questionnaire) some at least would have refused. 'In the end, we are secretly flattered when something without or against reason is asked or even demanded of us . . .'[27]

The same logic lies behind successful attempts at sexual seduction. If the seducer is too explicit in his demands, the object is likely to become wary or to refuse. Some mystery, at least, must remain. This is why we never usually tell someone we're attracted to straightaway that we fancy them and want to make love to them. Instead we ask them to go for a drink. The chances are that the person can guess why – but the point is they cannot be sure, and at least an element of challenge remains. Yet no matter how mysterious or even charming a challenge is, it by no means rules out unjust treatment. This is painfully clear from Søren Kierkegaard's *The Diary of a Seducer* (1843), dressed up as a classic seduction story, but actually a detailed account of the brutal humiliation of a young woman, just for the sake of it.

Johannes, the diarist, tells the story of how he seduced Cordelia simply because he wanted to mould and shape her as if she were a work of art. He finds her beautiful, but is not so much in love with her as with the idea of making her love him – or, more precisely, making her 'a victim of her own love'. Initially, by following her and observing her unseen (e.g. sneaking into her house and listening to her playing the piano) he is able to build up a portrait of her character. He is then confident of what will appeal to her. Feeling that to put himself directly in the position of suitor would be too obvious, he sets up a young wholesaler, Edvard Baxter, who is clearly in love with Cordelia, to do the job instead. While Baxter courts Cordelia Johannes subtly manipulates her feelings against him on the sidelines. When he senses that Edvard is about to declare his love to her, Johannes asks for her hand in marriage. She accepts.

Once Cordelia has accepted his marriage proposal, his first step is to teach her about love by acting so smitten by her that she will see how deeply love can affect a person. Sure enough the same feelings are instilled in her, as well as a conviction about the power she wields over Johannes. Yet just at the moment when her passion is at its height, Johannes suddenly withdraws from her. He appears preoccupied when they are together. He stops writing her love letters. Worried, she tries to 'recapture' him by using her newly learned erotic skills, but Johannes resists. Eventually, just as he has planned, she breaks off the engagement. His seduction of her is now complete. It is she who has led herself astray. She has voluntarily given herself to him, then voluntarily broken off the engagement herself. The final 'triumph' is that, thanks to some carefully laid hints by Johannes, she becomes fully aware of the extent of her seduction by him.

This systematic persecution is close to stalking. Conversely, stalking is like an act of seduction gone wrong, seduction without its paradoxical defining move of coercing someone to act freely. History recalls Lord Byron as seducer and Lady Caroline Lamb as a desperate unhappy lover. There's good reason for this, as her behaviour towards him was designed to force him to reciprocate or to humiliate him. But, at the same time, as a notorious seducer, were Byron's own techniques really so far away from stalking?

Because they resulted in the acquiescence of his targets (as they initially did with Lamb herself), they are not perceived as stalking. The bitter irony of this, from Lamb's point of view, is made clear in her novel *Glenarvon* (1816) – retitled, more dramatically, in the 1860s, *The Fatal Passion* – which portrays her affair with Byron, but makes the Byron figure, Ruthven Glenarvon, a figure who harasses a woman once she fails to return his love.

Up to a point stalking and seduction are two sides of the same coin, separated only by the kind of flimsy social protocols explored in films like *Following* and *Harry, He's Here to Help*. Every love affair requires that one party makes 'the first move', and this first move involves that person imposing their will upon another. As Slavoj Žižek puts it, 'there is no seduction which cannot at some point be construed as intrusion or harassment because there will always be a point when one has to expose oneself and "make a pass".'[28] There is always a 'moment of violence' which cannot be bypassed – and which may cause the recipient to take offence. Žižek's point suggests that stalking might legitimately be seen as a kind of sub-category of seduction, the extreme case which nevertheless serves to emphasize the various assumptions and illusions involved in its 'parent' category.

When we consider the similarity between stalking and seduction, classic literary seduction stories come to seem less like stories of obsessive love and more like accounts of mental and, at times, physical abuse. Samuel Richardson's monumental *Clarissa, or the History of a Young Lady* (1748–9), for example, tells a rather disturbing story about the prolonged efforts to seduce Clarissa Harlowe by the handsome rake and 'notorious woman-eater' Robert Lovelace. His attempts to win her over become first more devious (he helps her escape from her family and then 'protects' her by installing her in an upmarket brothel) and then more physical and violent. They culminate in him drugging and raping her. Thereafter Clarissa goes temporarily insane, having lost all the independence and power she had promised to enjoy following the inheritance from her father. Eventually she dies, perhaps having committed suicide.

Lovelace's treatment of Clarissa is a more literal version of what Johannes does to Cordelia in *The Diary of a Seducer*, a process he terms 'drugging her aesthetically'.[29] Both novels depict a systematic programme of manipulation, prosecuted with systematic patience, that is heavily suggestive of what we now call stalking. But at the same time, both novels expose some uncomfortable truths about love. For all the sadistic heartlessness of the protagonists, ultimately don't they attempt something that is natural to us all – to love in order to achieve some kind of self-gratification? Are we not simply less aware of or less open about this aim than Johannes and Lovelace? And, though there are obvious winners and losers in each of these novels, perhaps love is, at bottom, really a kind of game played by two participants, where each communication, each action, represents a 'move' or a set of tactics designed to manipulate the actions of the other towards us?

Clarissa is an epistolary novel, and one effect of this – and the sheer volume of letters – is that we are plunged directly into the psychodramas of obsessed people. Because there is no objective, omniscient narrator guiding us through the overall story, it is difficult to be sure what is *really* going on between the two main characters. What *Clarissa* amounts to is a series of narratives and counter-narratives. The shared details in Clarissa's and Lovelace's accounts, as well as the commentaries provided by Clarissa's main confidante, do clearly corroborate her view of events. But the note of uncertainty makes us recognize that, in love, reality is not always something objectively agreed upon.

A repeated refrain in Lovelace's letters is whether she really sees things as she says she does. He wonders, 'Whether her frost is frost indeed? Whether her virtue is principle? Whether, if *once subdued, she will not be always subdued?*'[30] His uncertainty about this is why he persists in what he sees as his attempts to win her over. Rape is envisaged by him as 'the ultimate trial' – the ultimate test of whether the way she appears to be *is* in fact how she feels; whether her 'no' really means *no* or is in fact a coded form of 'yes'. Of course this is convenient logic for a rapist. At the same time, though, the novel makes us realize that love is about the compatibility not of two people, but of two interpretations of reality. A successful relationship is simply one in which two people share the same illusion.

Love (and Other Delusions)

The fact is that there is something delusional about even what we consider 'normal' love. Pierre Bayard says that the way to defeat the cunning, rational-sounding delusions of paranoid thought disorder is by carefully identifying the points at which they subtly falsify reality. But he acknowledges that the problem is how to be sure when reality is actually being falsified. After all, this is not always easy in everyday life. Do we all agree, all the time, on what is occurring, *in reality*? It's especially obvious when it comes to the relationship between two people. What is the reality of any relationship? Even two people who love each other can disagree fundamentally about what is going on in their relationship. One may feel that the other depends on him, while that person might be equally convinced it is the other way around.

Freud regarded jealousy as an 'everyday' example of paranoia, something everyone is prone to. The most extreme kind of jealousy is 'delusional' jealousy, where someone becomes firmly convinced that a lover is being unfaithful and will not be swayed by any argument to the contrary, as in Shakespeare's *Othello*. This is akin to paranoia, for it consists of what Freud called 'delusions of reference', a mistaken conviction that a phrase or a gesture (e.g. a lover unintentionally touching another person) was referring to something other than it seemed.[31] This is another example of how the normal processes involved in loving someone skirt uncomfortably close at times to abnormal ones.

In his penetrating and rather strange book, *Love* (1822) – his own way of coming to terms with the experience of unrequited love – Stendhal portrays love as a phenomenon which, like paranoia or jealousy, involves transforming the real world into something else due to the interpretative endeavours of the mind. An integral part of the process of falling in love, he writes, is 'to overrate wildly, and regard [the beloved] as something fallen from Heaven'. He calls this phenomenon 'crystallization', comparing the process to the practice of throwing 'a leafless wintry bough' into a saltmine: 'Two or three months later they haul it out covered with a shining deposit of crystals. The smallest twig, no bigger than a tom-tit's claw, is studded with a galaxy of scintillating diamonds. The original branch is no longer necessary.' This is what happens in the mind of the lover. Crystallization 'is a mental process which draws from everything that happens new proofs of the perfection of the loved one'. When in love everything you think of or hear is absorbed into the process going on in your mind: 'You hear a traveller speaking of the cool orange groves beside the sea at Genoa in the summer heat: Oh, if you could only share that coolness with her!'[32] In a sense, what exists in the mind of the lover is really a fantasy version of the loved one, whose *real* body or personality is as unnecessary as the original pre-crystallized branch.

According to psychoanalysis, what we talk about when we talk about love is really fantasy. Choosing someone to love is a process governed by unconscious fantasies about what that person might be able to do for you and what you can give him or her in return. Love involves practical, realistic needs (for companionship, or sex, for example) but also desires which are staged by fantasy. After all, if it were just sex or a companion that we needed, we could make do with almost anyone. So why do we fall in love with a particular person? And why do we keep on loving them? The answer is fantasy. This is what lies behind our choice of a specific person to love. It accounts for the crystallization effect spoken of by Stendhal, the reason why we become so captivated by a loved one's name, say, or distinctive physical features. Love is what happens when a person comes to occupy the fantasy frame which has been designed and already installed in place so that desire can become realized. And what keeps lovers together is the binding power of the fantasies they create about each other.

Highsmith's novel *This Sweet Sickness* exposes this fantasy-dimension of love especially clearly by making it literal. Because of his unrequited love for Annabelle, David Kelsey leads a double life. Most of the week he lives under his own name in a modest boarding house, but at weekends he occupies another house in another town, under another name, which he has decorated and furnished so that it might appeal to Annabelle, and he imagines that he spends his time there with her. His second home functions as a literal 'fantasy-space' where he can live his life with Annabelle.

But the point about the novel is that this is only an extreme version of what we all do. Unrequited lovers naturally daydream about what it would be like if they were actually united with the object of their affection. Kelsey, like all Highsmith's protagonists, reminds us that, metaphorically, everyone leads a double life, living as ordinary law-abiding social beings in the real world, but *really* existing in our much more colourful fantasy life. The danger comes when, like him, we are unable to keep the two separate. At the end of *This Sweet Sickness,* responsible for two deaths, Kelsey fully assumes the identity of his alter-ego and lapses into full-blown psychosis. But love – 'normal' love – is so dependent on fantasy that keeping the two things separate is not always easy. It is perhaps a short step from the kind of 'lovesickness' we all happily acknowledge is part of being in love to the kind of 'sweet sickness' suffered by Highsmith's protagonist. To quote Bradley Headstone in Dickens's *Our Mutual Friend,* a man also unhinged by obsessive love, 'No man knows, till the time comes, what depths are within him. To some men it never comes; let them rest and be thankful!'[33]

In psychoanalytic terms, stalking is rooted in the inability to love in a *normal* way – that is, to be able to create a strong internal object image which is nevertheless independent from the self – an image which can consequently be *depended* upon. But it would be a mistake to assume that it follows from this that 'normal' love is free of negative impulses such as the need to control, to exploit, to manipulate, even to hate. Some philosophers who have considered love (e.g. Iris Murdoch, Max Scheler and Jules Toner)[34] assume that real love is one of the rare moments in our lives when we forget ourselves – that is, our basic egocentric existence – in order to empathize so completely with another being, someone who is 'not me'. Psychoanalysis, by contrast, insists that love – and by this it means 'normal', healthy, fulfilling love – is something which strengthens one's sense of identity through natural processes such as fantasy and narcissism.

As the psychoanalyst Jacques Lacan once put it, love 'can be mapped . . . only in the field of narcissism. To love is, essentially, to wish to be loved.'[35] It is nothing more than a powerful illusion which makes us feel that we are loving and being loved in return (i.e. giving something out and taking something back in) when in fact there is only one movement and it is the attempt to *take*. When we fall in love we imagine that a powerful involuntary attraction has issued forth from us and has alighted on an object. Yet in fact this movement is intended to trap the other's love and ensure that we are *loved*. Love, in this conception, is close to seduction – and also to the impulse that lies behind stalking. It is an effort to persuade someone else to love *us* – and this is what we really need to talk about when we talk about love, and its connection to stalking.

CHAPTER FIVE

Stalking and Morality

To follow the other, to substitute oneself for him, to exchange lives, passions
and wills, to metamorphose oneself in the other's stead, is perhaps the only
way for man to finally become an end for man.

Jean Baudrillard, 'Please Follow Me' (1987)

Your Friendly Neighbourhood Stalker

Like many Marvel heroes, the story of Spider-Man is really a tale of
adolescent wish-fulfilment. Becoming Spider-Man enables an awkward,
put-upon young man to beat the bullies and impress the girl he loves by
assuming a new, powerful, persona. Much of the success of Sam Raimi's
version of the story, the 2003 film *Spider-Man*, is because it makes this
dimension of the story explicit, associating the superhero's capacity for
transformation directly with the idea of adolescence. Parker starts to
become a spider as he is becoming a man. The film is also more of a love
story than the originals. His transformation into Spider-Man means he can

eventually get the girl, Mary Jane ('MJ'). But the twist is that, at the end, he rejects her.

To understand why we need to acknowledge that the film has added another layer of meaning to the Spider-Man story. It presents him as a benign stalker figure. Parker watches, follows, finds out about the object of his love. Early in the film MJ is unnerved by his detailed knowledge of all her performances in school plays since she was a child. In a later scene she meets him in downtown New York after she has had an acting audition. She is surprised to see him there, and wonders how he knows about her audition. His reply, 'I was in the neighbourhood', is intended to sound casual, but would be sinister in another context – and he quickly has to admit he is not there by chance.

But Parker wins her over in the end, because of Spider-Man's power. Spider-Man is always 'in the neighbourhood', ready to protect. Parker thus represents the 'desired intimate' stalker's ultimate fantasy: being recognized by the woman he pursues until she becomes as obsessed with him as he is with her, thus vindicating his obsession. The key scene comes after Spider-Man has saved MJ from possible gang-rape in an alleyway. As he hangs upside-down in the alleyway she tells him 'You have a knack for saving my life. I think I have a superhero stalker.' In a heavily overdetermined erotic moment, MJ peels down the mask and kisses his lips, as it pours down with rain.

This image is a visual summing-up of all the libidinal energy which the film (and its viewers) invests in the fantasy of transformation. In his tight-fitting red and blue-veined bodysuit, Spiderman of course resembles a penis. But his real power comes from the fact that he endows Parker with the power of what Freud called the 'phallus' – an ordinary object with surprising transformative potential. Ultimately, the stalker's fantasy is taken to its logical conclusion at the end of the film, once Parker is given the chance to reject MJ's declaration of love. Officially he does so so he can remain free to pursue his moral goals. But it means that the tables have turned and the superhero stalker is able to exact a subtle revenge for MJ's earlier inaccessibility.

This odd conflation of one of the ultimate cinematic heroes, the superhero, with one of its ultimate villains, the stalker, may seem bizarre, but in fact it just makes more obvious an ambivalence about the figure of the stalker which is often to be found in cinematic depictions of stalking. A number of films stop short of portraying the stalker as an outright heroic moral avenger, like Spider-Man, but they do treat him as a more ambiguous crusader who is out to change someone's life for the better. Such films invite us, either consciously or unconsciously, to side with the stalker or at least to recognize that there is a grim moral justification for his quest. Screen stalkers are figures worthy of fear and revilement, but they also demand our pity and empathy in ways that make it hard to simply dismiss them as evil. In *The Fan*, for example, Gil Renard's failed relationship with his son is one motivation behind his terrorizing of Bobby Rayburn. It results in Rayburn reassessing his life and realizing what is most important is something he has taken for granted, namely his supportive family. Sy Parrish in *One Hour Photo* exposes David Yorkin's infidelities to his wife Elena out of a sense of outrage that someone could be so lucky to be at the heart of a loving family, yet so casually able to abuse this privilege.

The black comedy *Harry, He's Here to Help* takes the theme further. Harry Balestrero is more than simply a weirdo with an acute sense of morality whom Michel Pape has had the misfortune to meet, but nothing other than a dark angel of destiny, who gradually, systematically, exposes the faultlines in Michel's life and solves his various 'problems' – from simple ones, like his clapped-out car (he buys him a shiny new 4x4) to complex ones, such as the unfair demands his family place upon him (Harry murders his parents and his brother). Of course there is a dangerous side to this, for Michel becomes possessed by Harry's demonic energy, almost to the point of going along with Harry's plans to do away with his wife and children, before coming to his senses and killing Harry instead.

But this is something too which, paradoxically, Harry has *enabled*, by forcing Michel to stop drifting through his life and evaluate what, and who, is important.

Stalkers in the movies (and in literature) are people who bring drastic change to people's lives, sometimes as an excessive, inappropriate punishment, but sometimes undoubtedly for the better. This is incongruous with real-life accounts of stalking, of course, which make it clear that the experience of being stalked can shatter a victim's life, making her or him reassess everything in it – friends, lovers, society, public space – and any 'good' that may come from this reassessment comes at a heavy price. Nevertheless the preoccupation with morality in stalking films is in keeping with the nature of stalking as a real-life behaviour. No one could be mistaken about the malicious intent of stalking, nor its destructive effects, yet it is clear that scarcely far from the surface in the mindsets of all stalkers – however misguided or deluded they may be – is a sense that they have been morally wronged, or that their victims deserve to be punished for moral failings.

Robert Fine notes that the original Latin term *persequor*, from which our modern 'persecution' is derived, means 'to pursue justice to the end'.[1] The actions of the three main categories of stalker are motivated, to varying degrees, by this notion of justice. 'Former intimates' typically feel that they have been rejected unfairly by a lover and are desperate to teach them what they have done wrong. 'Non-intimate' stalkers frequently act out of a conviction that someone has insulted them personally or are more generally 'getting away with' something they shouldn't. And though 'desired intimate' stalkers begin by idealizing their target, when this turns to defilement the justification is often moral – a moral imperative which is especially clear in the case of celebrity stalkers, who usually seek to punish their victims for their perceived hypocrisy or aloofness.

Besides vengeance, some stalkers regard themselves, perversely, as engaged in beneficial activities and complain about not receiving recognition for the time and effort they expend on the other person. Jeremy Dyer, whose lengthy correspondence with the victim of his stalking, TV presenter Sarah Lockett, exhibits a strange self-consciousness about his status as stalker (and who was found to be writing a guide on how to stalk when police raided his lodgings), referred to himself as her 'guardian stalker'. He told her: 'Oh well, there are good stalkers and bad stalkers and you, my dear, are lucky enough to get a good one who sends you nice presents and writes you nice things.'[2]

The victims of stalking are of course unlikely to feel persuaded by the stalker's moralizing, for the reality is that they are put through an ordeal which is painfully unjust. But inevitably, part of the reflex self-scrutiny occasioned by being a victim of stalking is an ethical reassessment of their actions: have I acted wrongly? *Have* I treated him unfairly? Victims may even feel they have offended another, more mysterious, kind of law which they, like Kafka's Josef K., simply cannot fathom. Fine likens the woman who persecuted him for over two years to the ancient Greek 'furies', the goddesses of vengeance, whose duty was to pursue and wreak revenge on those who had violated the law – ancient, ethical or actual state law – whether they knew it or not. He felt as if his stalker was punishing him according to a mysterious yet powerful law that operated in a different realm from the public laws that prevail in our society. By taking her to court he effectively had to set one form of justice against the other.

Identifying with the Stalker

What exactly causes us to empathize with stalkers on the screen? Much of it is down to the unique properties of the 'moving picture' as an art-form. There's an obvious parallel between stalking behaviour and the way the camera pursues and lingers over characters unobserved, *tracking* them. Cinema, as Orit Kamir says, 'trains viewers in voyeuristic stalking'.[3] This means that the numerous film sequences which detail the experience of following or being followed (such as Fritz Lang's *M* [1931], Jacques Tourneur's *Cat People* [1942], or Hitchcock's *Vertigo*) automatically make us feel as if we are *participating* in the unnerving activity of pursuit rather than simply observing it.

Film as a medium also involves a mechanism of viewer-identification which is more emotive and direct than other arts, and has significant implications when it comes to considering films about stalking. The cinematic apparatus – the huge screen, the dark auditorium, the larger-than-life characters, the bright colours, the crystal-clear soundtrack – means that going to the cinema is like entering one's own private fantasy-space. What we watch on screen seems somehow to be *about* us, we become involved in what we see, the camera stands in for our own eyes. Not surprisingly, many film theorists have explained the effect of watching a film by turning to the psychoanalytic theory of how fantasy 'stages' desire in our psychic life. The cinema screen, they argue, is a literal version of the unconscious fantasy-screen upon which we project our desires.

Film theory has long been fascinated by the way film 'positions' us as we watch, the way it manipulates us into identifying with the characters in different situations. As in personal unconscious fantasy – which is by no means a straightforward process of wish-fulfilment, as psychoanalysis insists, because the fantasizer doesn't consistently play the role of hero or heroine of a story – the viewer occupies a range of different, fluctuating 'subject positions' as the film progresses, which can complement or contradict one another. We can identify with a range of different characters at different moments, or even the same moment.[4]

The best, because least subtle, example of how this works with regard to stalking is the 'slasher' film. The murderer in this genre is either a supernatural killer, back from the dead (as in *Friday the 13th*, or *Nightmare on Elm Street*) or a more realistically portrayed sociopath who nonetheless has an almost supernatural ability to appear at will and to remain immune to attempts to kill him (as in *Halloween*). But his duty, to put it simply, is to

punish teenagers for moral weakness. In the classic slasher movies of the late 1970s and 1980s (*Halloween, When a Stranger Calls, He Knows You're Alone, Prom Night*, etc) this means sex. The body count in *Halloween* is dictated by the law that your chances of surviving a serial killer run in inverse proportion to your sexual experience. All of Michael Myers's victims are slain after having or during sex, as if they are being punished for their promiscuity or even their sexual desire. Only Laurie, ironically the apparent intended victim of the stalker, survives. Naturally *she* is a virginal figure, mocked by her sexually aware friends for being more of a babysitting 'girl scout' than a girl with an eye for the boys. It is no accident that throughout the film she has been able to catch glimpses of the figure of the stalker as he lurks around the neighbourhood, where Annie, her promiscuous friend, misses him or doesn't recognize him for what he is.

Laurie is an example of the slasher convention Carol Clover calls the 'Final Girl'.[5] This character, the main one in the film, is the only one of the group to survive. She is severely distressed by her ordeal, usually wounded, but the one who is ultimately able to confront the killer and win. Her great virtue, Clover thinks, is that, in a departure from the usual logic of horror movies, she is *both* victim *and* protagonist, and can thus be identified with by all viewers, female and male (e.g. in allowing male viewers to acknowledge their secret fears of being a victim). As such the slasher film complicates one of the most resonant arguments in film studies, Laura Mulvey's theory that most films require the viewer, whether male or female, to occupy the position of transcendent *male* subject and reduce the woman on screen to simply an object of his male gaze. The teen slasher film thus seems rather improbably feminist, for its women function as both 'suffering victim and avenging hero'.[6]

This is true of one of the more notable recent additions to the genre, *I Know What You Did Last Summer* (1997). But here the moral vengeance meted out by the stalker relates to more than just sex. The film details the stalking of four teenagers who have killed a fisherman while celebrating their graduation and the Fourth of July, and have made a pact to cover up the evidence and keep it a secret in order to save their futures. The fisherman apparently returns from the dead and persecutes the members of the group using strategies reminiscent of real-life stalkers: leaving written messages and symbolically charged reminders (e.g. live crabs in the back of a car covering a corpse), cutting the hair of one of the girls while she sleeps and scrawling 'SOON' in lipstick on her mirror. The fishing symbolism emphasizes the way he reels his victims in one by one as if they were fish.

This figure plays the role of moral avenger more directly than other films in the teen slasher genre. He sets out to punish the teenagers for their immorality – their arrogant assumption that they can literally get away with murder. As privileged (intelligent, good-looking, affluent) members of society they assume that a mere fisherman can reasonably be sacrificed to protect their deserved success. His vengeance causes them to reassess this assumption. In the end, with a dubious moral logic, they decide that because their persecutor is the man they thought they had drowned, they are not guilty of murder after all, for he has clearly survived. But he is not really out to avenge his near-death. Their *real* crime – thinking they have it all – is what he is out to punish.

This film emphasizes the uncomfortable fact that stalking in the slasher film, however terrifying and extreme, is to be understood by the viewer as *justified*, to some degree. Slasher films suggest that, for all the real-life findings of clinicians and lawyers about the devastating effects of stalking on its victims, cinema seems tacitly to endorse the perspective of the stalker, and imply the victim is somehow to blame. As viewers, we are cinematically implicated in this outcome, too, not just because of the tracking camera's capacity to get us to shadow the stalker but because, as Clover says, the perspective switches frequently between stalker and victim.

But it's actually more complex than this, for as well as occupying two different subject-positions, we are actually viewing the victim in two different ways from the *same* position, the stalker's. In this way cinema displays the familiar attitude towards the other person which is typical of pathological narcissism, veering between idealization and devaluation. We elevate the heroines, played by young actresses culturally regarded as desirable (Jamie Lee Curtis in *Halloween*, Sarah Michelle Gellar and Jennifer Love Hewitt in *I Know What You Did Last Summer*) to an idealized position whereby we admire them and, to an extent, empathize with them. At the same time, we are made to devalue them, becoming complicit in their persecution, and made to feel that it is somehow justified for what they have done or who they are. These girls thus occupy both sides of the narcissistic 'double fantasy' which underpins cultural depictions of stalking, the 'stabilizing' and the 'destabilizing' dimensions.

Reviewers have often commented that the characters in films like *I Know What You Did Last Summer* are too dislikeable to sympathize with. But this is precisely the point. Wholly sympathetic characters would not conform to the ambivalent logic of stalking; as it is, we have characters who are *superficially* attractive but repellent deep down. This ensures that we act

as narcissistic viewers, relating to another person as if she is both excessively attractive and excessively dislikeable.

Once we see how it works, it's natural to wonder how we can tolerate
this empathy with evil or unsavoury characters. The answer is, first, to
remind ourselves that it works primarily at an unconscious level. But, in
any case, don't we all, at times, harbour unpleasant, hostile feelings towards
others, which would embarrass or shame us if they were made public? This
is really the subtext of *Harry, He's Here to Help*. Harry is an embodiment of
Michel's 'id', whose duty is to act out the desires Michel needs to keep
repressed in order to function normally in society. Unconsciously, in a
Freudian sense, it would be understandable if Michel wished his parents
were dead, for they are a burden to him. Perhaps at times he even, though
he could not admit it to himself, wishes his children and wife were not such
a drain on his energy. Harry divines these secret feelings and acts on them
on Michel's behalf. Watching stalking on screen can perform a similar
function, providing us with an unconscious, safe, imaginary way of acting
out our aggressive desires. Once again we're reminded that the factors that
produce stalking behaviour in certain people – the narcissistic linking
fantasy, disappointment at rejection, the need to be loved – are *normal*
ones. It's just a question of what happens next, how we respond to them.

Outside the slasher genre, in films like *The Fan* or *Harry, He's Here to
Help*, encouraging the viewer to identify with the stalker is a more straightforward process, and is achieved by emphasizing, at key points, the
vulnerability of a person we could otherwise easily dismiss as demonic. This
is what makes the stalker just like us. It surely accounts for the enduring
appeal of *Taxi Driver*, where our relationship with Travis Bickle is much
more ambivalent than with a superhero like Spider-Man or the protagonists
of the vigilante movies of the 1970s (such as *Death Wish*) which the film
resembles. We are not asked to approve of what he does. But nevertheless
we come to identify with him, mainly due to his vulnerability. He appears to
be an innocent in a dark world. He is unable to tell when people (Betsy,

Sport) are being ironic. His integrity and his innocence are what attract Betsy and Iris to him, and it is what we respond to, too. Thus the film, to an extent, makes us empathize with his stalking mentality. The reason *Taxi Driver* is so powerful – and the reason it makes some critics very uneasy – is explained by Scorsese himself, who comments that 'The key to the picture is the idea of being brave enough to admit having these feelings, and then act them out. I instinctively showed that the acting out was not the way to go, and this created even more ironic twists to what was going on.'[7]

This dimension of stalking culture means that although on one level stalking films highlight the flimsiness of the tacit laws which structure everyday existence, on another they uphold a kind of implicit moral law. They thus partly conform to a strain within Hollywood and popular culture founded on the fantasy of revenge, a resurrection of the Jacobean and Elizabethan tradition of the 'revenge drama'. Modern cinematic examples include *Taxi Driver*, *Thelma and Louise*, almost all of Clint Eastwood's films (both as director and lead) from *Beguiled* to *Mystic River*, the 1993 film *Falling Down*, Tarantino's *Kill Bill*. It is significant that an emphasis should be placed on the implicit moral code in such films, and recent stalking movies, for what postmodern culture conspicuously lacks is a set of universally adhered to moral values.

Stalking, as I have argued, is a symptom of narcissistic culture. And in a narcissistic culture it follows that we are more inclined to take things *personally*. The judgements we make might really be narcissistic rage dressed up as moral outrage. Like the stalker, there is a tendency for people now to base their moral judgements not on a system of universally agreed ethical norms but on a much more partial and volatile personal moral code. One of Slavoj Žižek's recurring refrains in his analysis of postmodern culture is that while on the face of it the Western world is more liberal and democratic than ever, a rigid and unspoken set of moral rules in fact operates under the surface, maintaining strict limits as to what we are allowed to say or even to feel (or dictating what we *ought to* feel – as exemplified in the imperative to 'grieve' publicly following the death of figures such as Princess Diana, Pope John Paul ıı, George Best). In this sense we are culturally, to use Žižek's term, 'post-Oedipal', beyond the pleasure principle. It means that the moral criteria which dictate our society are not objective, universally agreed upon rules, as if outlined and maintained by an authoritative 'Oedipal' father-figure, but flexible 'recommendations', determined by individual, subjective desires.[8]

Final Girls and Fatal Women

Something we can't overlook here, though the decline of universal moral norms applies to both men and women, is the fact that the victims in all the films we have considered so far are women. For all her courage and ultimate success, the Final Girl is still a girl and the stalker figure a man – just like the majority of real-life stalking cases. Indeed Hollywood's notorious misogyny is readily visible in films which depict stalking.

A typical example, one which doesn't depend on subtle techniques of viewer-identification but hammers home its message crudely, is the 1991 film *Sleeping with the Enemy*. This is the story of a woman who, like a domesticated female equivalent of Travis Bickle, would not take it any more. Pushed to breaking-point by her possessive husband, Laura Burney fakes her death in a boating accident and begins a new life. But her husband Martin hunts her down and she is forced to kill him in self-defence. However, a moment of dark irony at the very end suggests that this still doesn't mean she has escaped him. As she embraces her new partner, the ring that symbolized her marriage to Martin glistens in the foreground, as a resounding 'ping' is heard on the soundtrack. Thus the vengeful husband's side of the story receives official endorsement, for his justification for his behaviour has always been the sanctity of the marriage bond.

Not all representations of female stalking work so conservatively, however. In fact, one of the more surprising aspects of the emphasis on justice in stalking films is that some films seem implicitly to take the woman's side. A key example is François Truffaut's *The Story of Adèle H.* (1975). On the face of it, this is an accurate depiction of a genuine nineteenth-century case of erotomanic stalking: the persecution of a British naval lieutenant by Victor Hugo's daughter, Adèle. On closer inspection it is much less straightforward. To begin with, Adèle's obsession – for all its recklessness and irrationality – is not entirely delusional. It is clear that before travelling to Canada Lieutenant Pinson had seduced her, promising marriage, and causing her to break-off her engagement to a famous poet. Besides the emotional impact, reneging on a deal like this had severe implications for a woman's social status in the mid nineteenth century.

Pinson's culpability is underlined by the fact that he is portrayed by director Truffaut (and the actor, Bruce Robinson) as an unremittingly charmless and uncaring man. This makes Adèle's obsession even more difficult to understand and enhances the bleakness of the story. Yet the point is undoubtedly that her pursuit of an unrewarding ideal makes her actions seem almost noble and stoic, the equivalent of the stoicism of the religious and political martyrs that interested Truffaut in other films. *The Story of Adèle H.* is careful to emphasize Victor Hugo's significance as a champion for the oppressed and exploited. As a defiant member of both groups his daughter is his equal in this respect. And, significantly, this casts her apparent erotomania in a radically different light. It may be delusional, but is also evidence of her unwavering faith and commitment to an ideal. Alternatively, maybe erotomania is like hysteria (a similarly contested term in medical history, erroneously associated mainly with women) in that it is really a historically specific form of protest at the social position a woman has been forced to adopt?

Upon its release the film critic Michael Klein argued that what is significant about *The Story of Adèle H.* is that its heroine attempts to play the role of a man. She is 'a romantic heroine who dares to act like Byron or

Shelley. She appears bizarre because nineteenth century romantic culture granted this role only to men.'9 A similar message might be buried deep within *Play Misty For Me*, for all its appearance to the contrary. What scares male viewers is the film's suggestion that any man can be vulnerable to persecution, even someone physically and mentally strong, and used to handling complicated sexual relationships. In this it is a typical product of the Hollywood 1970s, when events like the rise of feminism and the end of Vietnam were causing social anxiety. Clint Eastwood has described Garver as 'a free guy' and said that the intrigue of the film is the question, 'how does a free guy get manipulated like that?'10 The answer is that the particular notion of freedom Garver adheres to is no longer valid in the face of a new kind of danger represented by Draper – a woman comfortable playing the role of sexual predator, once reserved exclusively for a man. The film emphasizes this by making Draper more and more masculine throughout the film. By the end she is wearing trousers and her short hair has become even shorter. She dies after Garver punches her full in the face, as he would a man.

Yet from our contemporary post-feminist perspective, it is difficult not to see what happens to Garver as a form of retribution. His indifference towards most things might be the epitome of 1970s cool at one level, but it is downright cold-hearted on another. And though Draper's character is an expression of a prevailing cultural fear of women who act like men, the film also implies that Garver's attitude is becoming untenable at this point in history. Might what happens to him be regarded as no accident, at best, and, at worst, payback for his unenlightened attitude? It would be perverse to pretend that Evelyn Draper reacts as a *normal* woman would or should. But her behaviour also reflects on Garver's status as 'a free guy'. What is freedom? What does it entitle him to do? The implication is that our relationships with others always involve a certain kind of moral imperative, a responsibility to take into account another person's feelings and point of view.

A more recent stalking text underlines this shift in the nature of sexual politics by moving this theme from unconscious subtext to main story. Helen Zahavi's feminist novel *Dirty Weekend* (1991) is a notable addition to the late 1980s/1990s genre of 'serial killer' novels, for it features a female serial killer. Bella is being terrorized by a man who watches her outside her window and makes telephone calls, threatening 'I'm going to give you what you deserve.'[11] She decides she will take revenge on behalf of women like her who are terrorized by men simply because they are more physically powerful and require an outlet for their sexual desire. So she gives him what *he* deserves, breaking into his home and beating him to a pulp with a hammer. He is the first of a number of men killed by her as punishment for their sexual attitudes towards women.

Bella's stalker is described as her 'fate' because she is fated to wake up one day and realize 'she'd had enough'. His behaviour makes her realize the role she is destined to play, as self-appointed *femme fatale*. The idea of fate recurs continually in stalking stories, from *Our Mutual Friend* to *One Hour Photo*. In fact, the title of the film *Fatal Attraction* provides a shorthand summary of the way the theme works. The fatal attraction of stalking is like that of the *femme fatale* – 'fatal' not just in the sense that it can lead to death, but in the sense that stalking and its outcome somehow seems to be a character's fate, their destiny. The double logic is most literally portrayed in Muriel Spark's 1959 novel, *Memento Mori*, which tells the story of an old people's home which is being terrorized by phone calls in which the caller says simply 'Remember you must die'. One after another, members of the house meet their end. For much of the novel it seems to signal that the novel belongs to the Agatha Christie style 'clue-puzzle' detective story. It turns out, though, in an ironic supernatural twist, that the message is from none other than 'death' itself, simply stating a fact. This dimension of stalking novels and film is a kind of philosophical counterpart to the narrative suspense involved in stalking, that most escalatory of crimes. Just as the narrative is destined to lead inexorably to a dramatic endpoint from the first encounter between stalker and victim, so reading about or watching people being subjected to a stalking ordeal means that we sense they are about to face severe existential consequences as a result of their experience.

The Implications of Stalking

In real life, lest we forget, this process is a tortuous and unwelcome one. The victim of stalking has the morbid conviction that they are fated to meet their stalker at any moment. Being shadowed forces them to think of who they are, how they appear to others, what they do each day, in a new light. Even their sense of time changes, for stalking, as experts have stressed, is not 'linear' but 'cyclical' and repetitive. But although stalking films impress upon us how destructive and painful this process can be, cultural representations of stalking often undertake an ironic exploration of another, more positive, side to this.

Part of the black comedy in *Harry, He's Here to Help* is its lesson that, potentially, no one can know you better than the person who stalks you. Not even your mother or father, husband or wife, keeps track of your day-to-day activities with the same dedication. Harry seems to know Michel better than he does himself. The plot of the film is an answer to the mischievous question: would it be possible for any good to come of such a situation?

Marc Behm's twisted-detective novel *The Eye of the Beholder* agrees enigmatically that it would. The Eye's obsession with the serial killer Joanna Eris, whom he secretly follows across America as she commits her murders, means their relationship is founded on their shared sociopathy. But there is something genuinely touching about their relationship too, even though she is unaware of his presence, and they barely meet. As they move root-lessly from state to state they establish a routine that resembles the comfortable life of those who have been married for years. Each night, they 'meet up' again after the day's 'work', he secreted outside her window 'home again',[12] she relaxing within, cooking dinner, listening to records.

For all its undoubted perversity the Eye's devotion seems to spring from genuine, altruistic love. As Joanna becomes more and more of an outcast when her money, good fortune and youthful looks begin to run out, the Eye looks after her more demonstratively, sending her – anonymously – a birthday present to cheer her up, giving her coded warnings about the proximity of the FBI investigation, and framing two agents who were getting too close. The novel ends as Joanna flees the FBI in her car at high speed, pursued by the Eye. She crashes her car and dies but not before she is able to smile at him with a flicker of recognition.

Thus the novel presents us with an example of the closest thing to 'benign' stalking, if such a thing could exist. Hypothetically speaking, if a person were followed by someone every minute of every day, someone who was able to look out for them, yet without making their presence known, isn't it true that they would be guaranteed an extra degree of safety over most people who are forced to go about their daily business more or less alone? Of course, the Eye does what he does because he is compelled to psychotically. The reality of being followed at all times could never be anything but deeply unpleasant, and were she aware of her shadow Joanna would no doubt have acted differently. Yet the real point about the relationship in *The Eye of the Beholder* is that it is a desperate attempt to form an attachment with another human being by an intensely lonely individual in a world without love. The Eye's loneliness may be to do with his personal failings (his marriage has broken down), but is implicitly a consequence of the bleak *noir* world he inhabits.

In fact, it's not altogether true to say that this situation is purely hypothetical. Contemporary art provides real examples of people shadowing another as obsessively as the Eye. Vito Acconci's *Following Piece* is only the first example of stalking becoming incorporated directly into aesthetic practice. Laura Blereau turned the tables on Acconci and followed *him* in her 2001 video piece, *Following Vito*. Christina Ray and Lee Walton's *Following the Man of the Crowd* project in 2004 involved both artists tracking a series of strangers for 24 hours. Most extreme of all was Sophie Calle's *Venetian Suite* (1988), which documents her pursuit of a man from Paris to Venice, where she tailed him for 13 days, compiling an extensive dossier about his movements and her experiences shadowing him, accompanied by photographs.

In one sense, these works are *real* acts of stalking, because they really took place. But they cannot be confused with the criminal activity of stalking for in each case the victim remained unaware of the project until it was over (some never knew). Legally, stalking cannot really be stalking if the victim is unaware of it, because the crime is, by definition, determined by its effect on the persecuted party. In any case the idea of the victim remaining unaware of what is being done to them would negate the whole point of stalking from the perpetrator's point of view, which is to teach the victim a lesson, to get revenge or simply recognition. But stalking-artists like Acconci and Calle were not interested in dramatizing stalking at all, but using the motif of following someone to highlight *philosophical* inferences to be drawn from exploring the relationship between one human being and another.

Though Acconci's *Following Piece* was a kind of updated version of Poe's 'Man of the Crowd' as well as a parody of the detective story, he was not interested in finding out about the people he shadowed. What attracted him instead, as the poem that accompanied his photographs made clear, is the establishment of what he called an 'adjunctive relationship' in which he simply 'added himself on' to another person and – ironically, for someone playing stalker – relinquished control:

I give up control
I don't have to control myself
I become dependent on the other person, I need that other person,
that other person doesn't need me.[13]

This fascination with surrendering control to a stranger is also there in Calle's *Venetian Suite*. Though devoid of Acconci's sociological ambition, *Venetian Suite* is perhaps the closest real-life equivalent to the form of 'benign' stalking depicted ambiguously in *The Eye of the Beholder*. Just as her quarry, 'Henri B.', remained unaware of Calle's pursuit, so she knew very little about who he really was. Yet she came to feel profoundly attached to him, almost as if she was his guardian angel.

For all the compulsive atmosphere of her project (Calle maintains throughout that she is powerless to resist the urge to follow) what is most remarkable about it is its self-discipline. Calle claimed that she was uninterested in Henri B. She was not in love with him, even though at times it felt like pursuing a lover. She did not intend to uncover his 'secret life'. She tried not to impose a narrative on her activities by wondering what the outcome might be. Nor did she even intend to produce a work of art, for the episode took place, she claims, before she considered herself to be an artist.[14] As a result she effectively *negated* her desire and her will, and surrendered these to the other.

This self-negation is central to the philosopher Jean Baudrillard's complex analysis of *Venetian Suite* in his essay 'Please Follow Me', which argues that the piece raises crucial questions about the nature of individual identity and our relationship to others. There is a kind of paradoxical game going on in *Venetian Suite*, where each participant is simultaneously free and independent *and* yoked slavishly to the other. Calle's pursuit of Henri B., Baudrillard argues, 'relieves him' of 'the reponsibility for his own life',[15] for it is as if *she* is responsible for him, like an anxious mother shadowing her child who has wandered away from home, thinking he is alone. And, paradoxically, this means that *she* is simultaneously relieved of the responsibility for her own life, too, for all her energies are channelled simply into the act of following the unpredictable movements of another.

The beauty of this game, for Baudrillard, is that it parodies one of the prevailing myths of Western culture: that we are unique, separate, autonomous beings, in charge of our own destiny. Our pretensions to uniqueness are made to seem ridiculous when we are doubled in this way, just like someone making fun of another by mimicking them. But, more seriously, our desires and will are what make us individuals and when these are negated so is our sense of individuality.

Calle's *Venetian Suite* perhaps also reads as a critique of *individualism*. Its simple choreography provides a powerful image of the fundamentally social nature of existence. It reminds us that even when we are alone, we need the other person. That other can be a threat, and our dependency upon others may be painful, but stalking culture can nevertheless provide at least a crumb of comfort in a narcissistic world where our relationship to the other is in crisis.

The value in the growing mass of artworks, books and films which deal with stalking, perhaps even the debate about it as a whole, is that it invites us to reconsider, by implication, our relationships with others. Fictional representations of stalking have a cathartic effect. As Aristotle said of tragedy, we watch the suffering of another so that we can feel relieved in the knowledge that others suffer a worse fate than us. With stalking, there is undoubtedly a disturbing side to this, an element of *Schadenfreude* teased out by the mechanisms of art – and it is an element that is most powerfully at work in the slasher movie, which so cleverly puts us in the position of stalker. But the point about catharsis isn't simply that we take pleasure in the misfortune of another, but that we end a book or a film full of a renewed appreciation of what is valuable in our *own* lives. In the case of stalking culture, we can be reminded of what is important about our relationships with those we love, need or admire, what we expect from them, how we treat them.

References

Introduction

1 Patricia Tjaden and Nancy Thoennes, 'Stalking in America: Findings From the National Violence Against Women Survey', National Institute of Justice: Centers for Disease Control and Prevention (April 1998).

2 Sylvia Walby and Jonathan Allen, 'Domestic Violence, Sexual Assault and Stalking: Findings from the British Crime Survey', Home Office Research Study 276 (June 2004).

3 Kristine K. Keinlen, 'Developmental and Social Antecedents of Stalking', in J. Reid Meloy, ed., *The Psychology of Stalking* (San Diego, CA, and London, 1998), p. 61.

4 Doreen Orion, *I Know You Really Love Me* (New York, 1997), pp. 115–16.

5 Orit Kamir, *Every Breath You Take: Stalking Narratives and the Law* (Ann Arbor, MI, 2001).

6 www.terrortrap.com.

149

One: What is Stalking?

1 M. Pathé and P. E. Mullen, 'The Impact of Stalkers on their Victims', *The British Journal of Psychiatry*, 170 (1997), p. 12.

2 J.C.W. Boon and Lorraine Sheridan, *Stalking and Psychosexual Obsession: Psychological Perspectives for Prevention, Policing and Treatment* (Chichester, 2002), p. xxii.

3 These examples: Oxford English Dictionary.

4 Thomas Harris, *The Silence of the Lambs* (New York, 1989), p. 111.

5 *Time Magazine*, 'Paparazzi on the Prowl', 14 April 1961.

6 Ibid.

7 Susan Sontag, *On Photography* (London, 2002), p. 55.

8 Cited in Orit Kamir, *Every Breath You Take: Stalking Narratives and the Law* (Ann Arbor, MI, 2001), p. 105.

9 Joel Norris, *Serial Killers: The Growing Menace* (New York, 1988).

10 *Newsweek*, 15 August 1977; *Washington Post*, 1 August 1977; *Washington Post*, 7 August 1977: cited in Kamir, *Every Breath You Take*.

11 Details of the Bardo case from Rhonda Saunders, 'The Legal Perspective on Stalking', in J. Reid Meloy, ed., *The Psychology of Stalking* (San Diego, CA, and London, 1998), p. 27; Doreen Orion, *I Know You Really Love Me* (New York, 1997), pp. 28–9, 67–8.

12 *US News and World Report*, cited in Kamir, *Every Breath You Take*, p. 123.

13 See, for example: *Newsweek*, 'Death of a Beatle', 22 December 1980; *Time Magazine*, 'The Last Day in the Life', 22 December 1980; *New York Magazine*, 'The Death and Life of John Lennon', 22 December 1980.

14 Stanley Cohen, *Folk Devils and Moral Panics* (London, 1972), p. 9.

15 E. S. Herold, D. Mantle and O. Zemitis, 'A Study of Sexual Offences Against Females', *Adolescence*, 53 (1979), pp. 65–72.

16 P. Taylor, B. Mahendra and J. Gunn, 'Erotomania in Males', *Psychological Medicine*, 13 (1983), pp. 645–50.

17 Ben Elton, *Blast from the Past* (London, 1999), p. 12.

18 M. A. Zona, K. K. Sharma and J. C. Lane, 'A Comparative Study of Erotomanic and Obsessional Subjects in a Forensic Sample', *Journal of Forensic Sciences*, 38 (1993), pp. 894–903; K. McAnaney, L. Curliss and C. E. Abeyta-Price, 'From Imprudence to Crime: Anti-Stalking Laws', *Notre Dame Law Review*, 68 (1993), p. 819; R. B. Harmon, R. Rosner and H. Owens, 'Obsessional Harassment and Erotomania in a Criminal Court Population', *Journal of Forensic Sciences*, 40 (1995), pp. 188–96; J. A. Wright, A. G. Burgess, A. W. Burgess *et al*, 'A Typology of Stalking', *Journal of Interpersonal Violence*, 11 (1996), pp. 487–502; P. E. Mullen, M. Pathé, R. Purcell, *et al*, 'Study of Stalkers', *American Journal of Psychiatry*, 156 (1999), pp. 1244–9.

19 Orion, *I Know You Really Love Me*; Robert Fine, *Being Stalked: A Memoir* (London, 1997); Gregory Dart, *Unrequited Love: On Stalking and Being Stalked* (London, 2003).

20 P. E. Mullen, M. Pathé, R. Purcell *et al*, 'Study of Stalkers', p. 1246.

21 Jean Laplanche and Jean-Bertrand Pontalis, 'Fantasy and the Origins of Sexuality' [1964], in Victor Burgin, J. Donald and C. Kaplan, eds, *Formations of Fantasy* (London, 1986), pp. 5–34.

22 Nick Hornby, *A Long Way Down* (London, 2005), p. 6.

23 The Network for Surviving Stalking: www.nss.org.uk, accessed 15 November 2005.

24 Dart, *Unrequited Love*, p. 27.

25 Sigmund Freud, 'On Narcissism: An Introduction' [1915], *The Penguin Freud Library*, vol. XI: *On Metapsychology* (London, 1991), pp. 65–97.

26 Otto Kernberg, *Borderline Conditions and Pathological Narcissism* (Northvale, NJ, 1990), p. 234.

27 Ibid., p. 236.

28 J. Reid Meloy, ' The Psychology of Stalking', in Meloy, *The Psychology of Stalking*, pp. 1–23, 18.

29 Ibid., p. 19.

30 Ibid., p. 21.

31 Gavin de Becker, *The Gift of Fear: Survival Signals that Protect us from Violence* (New York, 1997).

32 Kamir, *Every Breath You Take*, p. 8.

33 Patrick Hamilton, *The Siege of Pleasure*, in *Twenty Thousand Streets Under the Sky* (London, 2004), p. 291.

34 S. Gibbons, 'Freedom from fear of stalking', *European Journal on Criminal Policy and Research*, 6 (1998), pp. 133–41, 137

35 My thanks to Dr Berrios for this insight.

36 Philip Hensher, 'Bad News, Tracey, You Need Brains to be a Conceptual Artist', *The Independent*, 27 April 2001; Interview with Tracey Emin, *Observer Magazine*, 13 July 2003; Philip Hensher, 'Give Me a Break', *Spectator*, 16 August 2003; Amelia Hill, 'The Artist, The Critic and a War of Words', *Observer*, 17 August, 2003; Paul Bailey, 'Tracey Emin is Innocent', *Guardian*, 19 August, 2003; 'Tracey Emin: An Apology', *Spectator*, 13 September 2003.

37 P. E. Mullen, M. Pathé and R. Purcell, *Stalkers and their Victims* (Cambridge, 2000), p. 6.

Two: Stalking in Contemporary Culture

1 Geert Lovink, 'Civil Society, Fanaticism, and Digital Reality: A Conversation with Slavoj Zizek' (1996), www.ctheory.net, accessed 15 November 2005.

2 Details of Madonna case from Rhonda Saunders, 'The Legal Perspective on Stalking', in J. Reid Meloy, ed., *The Psychology of Stalking* (San Diego, CA, and London, 1998), pp. 37–9.

3 Details of Hinckley case from Richard J. Bonnie, John C. Jr. Jeffries and Peter W. Low, *A Case Study in the Insanity Defense: The Trial of John W. Hinckley, Jr.* (New York, 2000); 'The John Hinckley Trial: Transcript Excerpts', http://www.law.umkc.edu/faculty/projects/ftrials/hinckley,

accessed 15 November 2005.

4 Orit Kamir, *Every Breath You Take: Stalking Narratives and the Law* (Ann
   Arbor, MI, 2001), pp. 125–6.

5 Robert Fine, *Being Stalked: A Memoir* (London, 1997), p. 150.

6 Lorraine P. Sheridan, Eric Blaauw and Graham M. Davies, 'Stalking: Knowns
   And Unknowns', *Trauma, Violence and Abuse*, 4:2 (April 2003), p. 150.

7 Fine, *Being Stalked*, p. 130.

8 Nick Hornby, *A Long Way Down* (London, 2005), p. 6.

9 Christopher Nolan, '*Following* On: Christopher Nolan and Jeremy
   Theobald interviewed by James Mottram', in Nolan, *Memento and
   Following* (London, 2001), pp. 93–102, 96.

10 Fine, *Being Stalked*, p. 130.

11 Ibid., p. 31.

12 Nolan, '*Following* On', p. 97.

13 Cited in Susannah Clapp, 'The Simple Art of Murder', *The New Yorker*,
   10 December 1999, p. 95.

14 Ibid., p. 96.

15 T. Burt, K. Sulkowicz and K. Wofrage, 'Stalking and Voyeurism Over the
   Internet: Psychiatric and Forensic Issues', *Proceedings of the American
   Academy of Forensic Sciences*, 3 (1997), p. 172.

16 Richard Gallagher, *I'll Be Watching You: True Stories of Stalkers and Their
   Victims* (London, 2001), p. 125.

17 Saunders, 'The Legal Perspective in Stalking', pp. 25–49, 40–1.

18 Chris Rojek, *Celebrity* (London, 2001).

19 Gallagher, *I'll Be Watching You*, p. 76.

20 Entertainment Television International:
   www.eonline.com/Features/Specials/Stalkers, accessed 15 November 2005.

21 Rojek, *Celebrity*, p. 11.

22 See Henry Jenkins, *Textual Poachers* (London, 1992); Matt Hills, *Fan
   Cultures* (London, 2002).

23 Keith McKay, *Robert de Niro: The Hero Behind the Masks* (New York, 1986),

pp. 112–13.

24 Jillian McDonald, www.meandbillybob.com, accessed 15 November 2005.

25 E.g. Susan Kandel, 'Sherrie Levine: Stalker', *Art/Text*, 59 (Nov 1997/ Jan 1998), pp. 66–70.

26 Christopher Lasch, *The Culture of Narcissism* (New York, 1979), pp. 97, 92.

27 Kamir, *Every Breath You Take*.

Three: Enter the Stalker

1 J. Reid Meloy, ed., *The Psychology of Stalking* (San Diego, CA, and London, 1998), p. xix.

2 Glen Skoler, 'The Archetypes and Psychodynamics of Stalking', in J. Reid Meloy, ed., *The Psychology of Stalking*, p. 88.

3 P. E. Mullen, M. Pathé and R. Purcell, *Stalkers and their Victims* (Cambridge, 2000), p. 6.

4 Gregory Dart, *Unrequited Love: On Stalking and Being Stalked* (London, 2003), pp. 53, 60.

5 Charles Dickens, *Our Mutual Friend* [1865] (London, 2002), pp. 533–4.

6 Ibid., p. 536.

7 Ibid., pp. 388–9.

8 Michel Foucault, 'The Dangerous Individual', in *Politics, Philosophy, Culture: Interviews and Other Writings*, trans. Alan Sheridan (London, 1990), pp. 144, 149.

9 Orit Kamir, *Every Breath You Take: Stalking Narratives and the Law* (Ann Arbor, MI, 2001).

10 Ibid., p. 73.

11 Bram Stoker, *Dracula* [1897] (London, 1993), p. 439.

12 Walter Benjamin, *Charles Baudelaire: A Lyric Poet in the Era of High Capitalism*, trans. Harry Zohn (London, 1993), p. 48.

13 Edgar Allan Poe, 'Man of the Crowd' [1840], in *The Fall of the House of*

Usher (London, 1986), pp. 184, 188.

14 See, for example, John Plotz, *The Crowd: British Literature and Public Politics* (Berkeley, CA, 2000).

15 Charles Baudelaire, 'The Painter of Modern Life' [1863], in *Selected Writings on Art and Literature* (London, 1992), p. 403.

16 Dart, *Unrequited Love*, p. 118.

17 Slavoj Žižek, 'The Seven Veils of Fantasy', in Dany Nobus, ed., *Key Concepts of Lacanian Psychoanalysis* (London, 1998), p. 192.

18 Benjamin, *Charles Baudelaire*, p. 54.

19 See Janet Wolff, 'The Invisible Flâneuse: Women and the Literature of Modernity', *Theory, Culture and Society*, 2:7 (1985), pp. 37–46; Susan Buck-Morss, 'The Flâneur, the Sandwichman, and the Whore: The Politics of Loitering', *New German Critique*, 39 (Fall 1986), pp. 99–140; Griselda Pollock, 'Modernity and the Spaces of Femininity', in *Vision and Difference: Femininity, Feminism and Histories of Art* (London, 1988), pp. 50–90.

20 Cited in Benjamin, *Charles Baudelaire*, p. 39.

21 See Mark Seltzer, *Serial Killers: Life and Death in America's 'Wound Culture'* (London, 1998).

22 David Thompson and Ian Christie, eds, *Scorsese on Scorsese* (London, 1996), p. 62.

23 Susan Sontag, *On Photography* (London, 2002), p. 55.

Four: Stalking and Love

1 Raymond Carver, 'What We Talk about When We Talk about Love', in *What We Talk about When We Talk about Love* [1981] (London, 1993), pp. 114–29, p. 118.

2 Doreen Orion, *I Know You Really Love Me* (New York, 1997), p. 69.

3 Famous American Trials: The John Hinckley Trial 1982, www.law.umkc.edu/faculty/projects/ftrials, accessed 15 November 2005.

4 Robert Fine, *Being Stalked: A Memoir* (London, 1997), p. 17.

5 Robert Lipsyte, 'The Dangerously Thin Line of Fanaticism', *New York Times*, 29 June 1997.

6 Pierre Bayard, *Who Killed Roger Ackroyd?* (London, 2000), p. 89.

7 Mullen and Pathé, The Pathological Extensions of Love', *British Journal of Psychiatry*, 165 (1994), pp. 614–23, 619.

8 M. D. Enoch and W. H. Trethowan, *Uncommon Psychiatric Syndromes* (Bristol, 1979), p. 16.

9 Ibid., pp. 22–3.

10 Mullen and Pathé, 'The Pathological Extensions of Love', p. 620.

11 Orion, *I Know You Really Love Me*, p. 71.

12 Patricia Highsmith, *This Sweet Sickness* [1960] (New York, 2002), p. 91.

13 Enoch and Trethowan, *Uncommon Psychiatric Syndromes*, p. 33.

14 Ian McEwan, *Enduring Love* (London, 1998), p. 128.

15 G. E. Berrios and N. Kennedy, 'Erotomania: A Conceptual History', *History of Psychiatry*, 13 (2002), pp. 381–400.

16 D. A. Portemer, 'Les Érotomanes. Étude médico-légale' [1840], trans. G. E. Berrios, *History of Psychiatry*, XI (2000), pp. 435–43.

17 Michel Foucault, *Madness and Civilisation* (London, 1973), and *Discipline and Punish* (London, 1975).

18 William Jankowiak, ed., *Romantic Passion: A Universal Experience?* (New York, 1995), p. 4.

19 E.g. *I'll Be Watching You*, by Victoria Gotti (New York, 1998), Charles de Lint (New York, 2004) and Andrea Kane (New York, 2005); Ann Rule, *Every Breath You Take: A True Story of Obsession, Revenge and Murder* (2002); Richard Gallagher, *I'll Be Watching You: True Stories of Stalkers and Their Victims* (London, 2001); Orit Kamir, *Every Breath You Take: Stalking Narratives and the Law* (Ann Arbor, MI, 2001).

20 Glen Skoler, 'The Archetypes and Psychodynamics of Stalking', in J. Reid Meloy, ed., *The Psychology of Stalking* (San Diego, CA, and London, 1998), p. 110.

21 Doris M. Hall, 'The Victims of Stalking', in Meloy, ed., *The Psychology of Stalking*, p. 122.

22 J. Reid Meloy, 'The Psychology of Stalking', in Meloy, ed., *The Psychology of Stalking*, p. 7.

23 McEwan, *Enduring Love*, p. 95.

24 *The Onion*, 7 April 1999.

25 *Aftonbladet*, 10 October 2000, www.aftonbladet.se/nyheter/0010/10/agneta.html, accessed 15 November 2005.

26 Jean Baudrillard, *Fatal Strategies* (London, 1983), p. 103.

27 Jean Baudrillard, 'Please Follow Me', *Art and Text*, 23:4 (March–May 1987), p. 105.

28 Slavoj Žižek, 'You May!', in Bran Nicol, ed., *Postmodernism and the Contemporary Novel* (Edinburgh, 2002), p. 125.

29 Søren Kierkegaard, *The Diary of a Seducer* [1843] (London, 1999), p. 224.

30 Samuel Richardson, *Clarissa* [1748–9] (London, 1985).

31 Sigmund Freud, 'Some Neurotic Mechanisms in Jealousy, Paranoia and Homosexuality' [1922], *The Penguin Freud Library, vol. 10: On Psychopathology* (London, 1993), p. 207.

32 Stendhal, *Love* (Harmondsworth, 1975), pp. 45–6.

33 Charles Dickens, *Our Mutual Friend* [1865] (London, 2002), p. 389.

34 Max Scheler, *The Nature of Sympathy* [1913], trans. Peter Heath (London, 1954); Jules Toner, *The Experience of Love* (Washington, Cleveland, 1968); Iris Murdoch, *The Sovereignty of Good* [1970] (London, 1985).

35 Jacques Lacan, *Seminar XI: The Four Fundamental Concepts of Psychoanalysis*, trans. Alan Sheridan (Harmondsworth, 1986), p. 253.

Five: Stalking and Morality

1 Robert Fine, *Being Stalked: A Memoir* (London, 1997), p. 129.

2 Richard Gallagher, *I'll Be Watching You: True Stories of Stalkers and Their Victims* (London, 2001), p. 84.

3 Orit Kamir, *Every Breath You Take: Stalking Narratives and the Law* (Ann Arbor, MI, 2001), p. 79.

4 Elizabeth Cowie, 'Fantasia', *m/f*, 9 (1984), pp. 71–105.

5 Carol Clover, *Men, Women and Chainsaws: Gender in the Modern Horror Film* (London, 1992), pp. 39–40.

6 Ibid., p. 17.

7 David Thompson and Ian Christie, eds, *Scorsese on Scorsese* (London, 1996), p. 62.

8 Slavoj Žižek, *The Ticklish Subject: The Absent Centre of Political Ontology* (London, 1999); *Welcome to the Desert of the Real* (London, 2002).

9 Michael Klein, '*The Story of Adele H.*: The Twilight of Romanticism', *Jump Cut*, 10–11 (1976), pp. 13–15.

10 'Play it Again . . . A Look Back at *Play Misty For Me*', *Play Misty For Me* DVD version, Columbia Pictures/Sony Pictures Home Entertainment (2001).

11 Helen Zahavi, *Dirty Weekend* (London, 1991), p. 10.

12 Marc Behm, *The Eye of the Beholder* (Harpenden, 1999), pp. 93–4.

13 Vito Acconci, '*Following Piece*: Documentation of the Activity', Thomas Y. Levin, Ursula Frohne and Peter Weibel, eds, CRTL [SPACE]: *Surveillance Culture from Bentham to Big Brother* (Cambridge, MA, 2002), p. 405.

14 Sophie Calle, 'Sophie Calle in Conversation with Bice Curiger', in Adrian Searle, ed., *Talking Art 1* (London, 1993), p. 30.

15 Jean Baudrillard, 'Please Follow Me', trans. Paul Foss, *Art and Text*, 23:4 (1987), p. 106.

Acknowledgements

Thanks to everyone who told me they had come across some lurid tale of harassment and thought of me . . . This project was partly shaped by films or books recommended to me by friends and colleagues, and I'm grateful to each person who gave me a reference. Thanks also to the Centre for European and International Studies Research at the University of Portsmouth who awarded me funding to help me finish the research. I'm grateful to Ben Noys for reading an early draft and making such invaluable suggestions, and to the anonymous readers for Reaktion. Thanks, too, to Dr G. E. Berrios, Jillian McDonald and Harry Gilonis. Because the book dwells so much on misunderstood love, it was a relief to write it in a climate of real, nourishing love. So my special thanks to the three dedicatees: Karen Stevens for her support from start to finish, and to Joe and Jamie for always seeing the funny side.

List of Illustrations